A Philosophical Introduction to Theology

A Philosophical Introduction to Theology

J. Deotis Roberts

SCM PRESS
London

TRINITY PRESS INTERNATIONAL
Philadelphia

This edition first published 1991

SCM Press Ltd   Trinity Press International
26–30 Tottenham Road   3725 Chestnut Street
London N1 4BZ   Philadelphia PA 19104

© J. Deotis Roberts 1991

British Library Cataloguing in Publication Data

Roberts, J. Deotis (James Deotis) *1927–*
A philosophical introduction to theology.
1. Theology – Philosophical perspectives
I. Title
200.1

ISBN 0–334–02494–3

Library of Congress Cataloging-in-Publication Data

Roberts, J. Deotis (James Deotis), 1927–
A philosophical introduction to thelogy / J. Deotis Roberts.
p. cm.
ISBN 1–56338–006–4
1. Philosophy and religion–History. I. Title.
BL51.R575 1991
261.5′1–dc20   90–24500
CIP

Phototypeset by Input Typesetting Ltd
and printed in Great Britain by
Billings & Sons Ltd, Worcester

In memory of my son,
J. Deotis Roberts, Jr.

Contents

Preface

Several events led to the writing of this book. The quest for religious knowledge has been a lifetime endeavor. In recent years there has been an onslaught of anti-intellectualism in religious circles. At the same time, conservative religious groups have entered the public policy arena. This has had a retarding influence upon those who dare to think or believe in different ways. There is a need for leaders, including ministers, to be equipped to engage in critical thinking so as to guide others to clarity of thought and decision.

We in the West share a world-view largely shaped by ideas rooted in the Judeo-Christian and Greco-Roman heritage. As an Afro-American, I am aware of other roots—i.e. our African heritage. While I have written often of this latter influence, my concern here is the common heritage of ideas in the so-called First World.

This book is a modest attempt to provide a basic understanding of the manner in which our Western philosophical tradition has influenced theology.

When I was invited to teach theology at Eastern Baptist Theological Seminary in 1984, one course I offered as a requirement was the subject-matter of this text. During the years 1984–1986, I had the privilege of teaching this course to incoming students. This allowed me the privilege of sharing much but also learning much from students. During the years 1986–88, while serving as Commonwealth Professor at George Mason University, I sought every opportunity to research and compile the present manuscript. I am grateful to all who allowed or arranged this splendid opportunity for further reflection and writing.

In the meantime, other colleagues shared my conviction that philosophy has a place in the seminary and ministerial formation. Among these is Diogenes Allen, who produced a definitive study, *Philosophy for Understanding Theology*. It was also Allen who organized an ecumentical conference on the subject-matter of his book at Princeton Theological Seminary. I was fortunate to be invited to participate in this conference. The opportunity to trade experiences and ideas with colleagues in a common endeavor greatly aided me in my own project.

I take full responsibility for any weakness in this undertaking, but

I express profound thanks to all who have contributed to the effort. Eastern Baptist Theological Seminary provided generous financial support. Mrs Ruth Fox has again given the manuscript acceptable form. As always, my wife Elizabeth and my three daughters, Charmaine, Carlita and Kristina, have supported me with their love and understanding. My grandson, André, though only a year old, has reminded me of the wonder and joy of life.

If this book informs and inspires the reader to embark upon his/her own quest for religious truth, it will have served the purpose of my intention.

I

Introduction

In the Beginning

This is a philosophical introduction to theology. We need to know what we mean by philosophy and theology in order to establish their relationship in our study.

A philosopher is said to be one who loves wisdom. Philosophy is an activity of humans by virtue of their ability to think and their desire to know. Philosophy depends upon a critical or reflective attitude. Philosophy is based upon concepts and the formulation of principles and procedures of thought. It raises the question of meaning and the significance of the world in which we live. Every phase of human existence as well as the cosmos is within the province of philosophy. Philosophy reflects upon and interprets its subject-matter on the basis of available knowledge. Philosophical thought is at once analytic and speculative. The philosopher analyzes concepts and principles. He/She is prepared to examine the meaning of beliefs and values. The philosopher is concerned about the relation of ideas and their clarification.[1]

Theology has traditionally been defined as knowledge of God. That is to say, it is an attempt to reason or think about God or the Supreme Reality. Theology is partial to a particular religion or faith-claim. Philosophy is free to examine critically the idea or concept of God, while theology is related to a faith-affirmation in reference to a particular understanding of God. Hence there is a fundamental difference between Hindu theology and Christian theology. The difference is lodged in a belief system which undergirds a particular understanding of a supreme reality and a corresponding world-view and religious outlook.

Theology in this discussion is Christian in focus. Its meaning includes not just reasoning about God, but all that this implies in our understanding of the world. Theology is an intellectual pursuit which requires rigorous study in several cognate disciplines, including philosophy.

The relationship between philosophy and theology is very close. The traditions have developed along parallel lines that have often interfaced. Philosophers often treat theological subjects, and theologians often do their reflection out of philosophical schools. In fact, theologians often re-conceive the entire Christian creed through the use of ideas espoused by a particular philosopher. So important is this interaction between the two disciplines that I have called this study *A Philosophical Introduction to Theology*.

This is in some ways a hybrid study. It does not fit the usual classification of academic disciplines in the university or seminary. We need, therefore, to clarify the scope of our investigation. What I am attempting here is to bring the history of ideas and theological discourse together. I want to demonstrate how philosophy has been instrumental to theological reflection. But my primary goal is to understand theology.

Furthermore, I have special people in mind as I write. This is not a book to challenge those who have a good grasp of both disciplines, except to provide them with a new perspective. It is, rather, written with those in mind who have little or no direct exposure to the study of philosophy, but who will not be able to read widely in theological literature, with in-depth understanding, without upgrading their philosophical knowledge, upon which so much theology depends.

I do not assume, therefore, that we can plunge immediately into the goal of our study. We need to look at certain basic philosophical ideas before we can begin to use philosophy to do theological reflection. Certain foundational work must be done in philosophy before we will be able to arrive at the dialogue stage of our study. My experiences with seminarians, lay Christians and pastors have convinced me that there is a need for the resource provided by this study.

Diogenes Allen has made a noble attempt with a similar purpose in mind. I have used his text, but find that another approach is necessary for those who have little acquaintance with philosophy. Allen writes:

Instead of a brief presentation of philosophical thought which has been selected on the basis of what philosophers themselves find important and interesting, I have made my selection from the mass of philosophical material by first looking at *theologians*.[2]

It is Allen's opinion that by examining concepts and terms used by theologians from philosophy, he will be able to be most helpful to his readers. What he presents and the manner in which he presents it does not meet the needs of those who have no prior knowledge of philosophy. Philosophy is a very difficult discipline. It requires a certain mind-set to think as philosophers do or to understand what they are saying. Some prior knowledge of the discipline is needed to enter into meaningful conversation with them. If major theologians had not used philosophical ideas, we could do better, perhaps, without the effort to enter into the philosophical frame of mind. But since this is not the case, we need to find the best way to introduce their ideas to the uninitiated.

So I am attempting a different approach from that of Allen. This does not mean that I do not appreciate the major contribution he has made. I am aware of those needs he has not met. This study is an attempt to supplement his effort.

Here I will present some basic philosophical knowledge. I do so as one who has taught systematic theology for many years. At the same time my work in philosophy, philosophy of religion and philosophical theology has made me familiar with the history of ideas and the way these ideas have been used to interpret religious experience as well as in theological discourse. I view my task, however, as that of a theologian rather than a philosopher. I am aware of basic ideas used by theologians in building their systems of thought. I will first introduce the ideas as they were intended by those who formulated them. By first getting into the mind of the philosopher, we will understand better how as well as what he thinks. We will then be in a position to judge the validity of the appropriation of the philosopher's ideas by a particular theologian. What the philosopher thinks will be carefully critiqued from a theological point of view. We want to assess the value and validity of philosophical ideas for theological reflection. Our examination of philosophical ideas are from a theological point of view and for a theological purpose.

Any study of this dimension must be delimited in order to be manageable. In a time when such subject-matter requires a global vision and input, some statement needs to be made about the limits of our study. The study is clearly Western and Christian. It could be said to be mainly Protestant as well. My interest in comparative religions and contextualized and liberation theologies is well-known, but there can be only infrequent references to that broad interest here. From time to time the reader will be made aware of cross-cultural issues, but the special focus of this study will be honored. This is the inseparable relationship between philosophy and theology in the West.

Again, I need to say more precisely that this study is neither philosophy of religion nor philosophical theology. Philosophy of religion belongs more to philosophy than to theology. It is a critical and objective examination of religious ideas or concepts. It requires no faith affirmation on the part of the thinker. As a discipline, it is another branch of philosophy with a particular area of interest. Philosophical theology is a branch of theology. It is highly specialized. It may indeed include a faith-claim on the part of the thinker and often does. It assumes that one is acquainted with the two disciplines and has sufficient mastery of a particular philosophical position to rethink the creed of a particular religion. Existential and process theologies are examples of philosophical theologies.

It is obvious that neither philosophy of religion nor philosophical theology match our purpose in this study. Our study falls between the stools, as it were. It defies classification in our usual academic programs. It is neither philosophy nor theology. It is a philosophical introduction to theology, and it is a theological perspective on the use of philosophy for the doing of theology.

The method of this study will be dialogic. I wish to initiate a mutual conversation between philosophy and theology. My goal is that we shall end up with a knowledgeable and critical use of philosophical ideas in theological reflection and construction.

The procedure will be as follows: first, we will attempt to withhold any theological judgments until we have a reasonable grasp of a philosopher's point of view. In some sense we will want to sit at a philosopher's feet and hear him/her out. We really want to know what he/she thinks, especially on questions that are crucial to both fields. Our response will be a critical theological assessment of the validity of a particular philosophical point of view for our theological use. It is possible that we will need to say and no. We will examine various theological programs throughout history in which philosophical ideas have been used for theological reflection.

The study will be carried out so as to maximize our purpose. I assume very little philosophical or theological knowledge on the part of the reader. So I shall let the philosophers speak to us about questions we have in common. This is especially true in the formative period of Western philosophy. Next I shall show how philosophy has been incorporated into various theological programs throughout Christian history. Here we will be able to deal only with broad periods and representative thinkers. Finally I shall demonstrate the relation between philosophy and theology through discussion of specific projects, e.g. the personalism of the Boston School of Theology. The reader will now be prepared for serious study in philosophy of religion, systematic theology or philosophical theology. The purpose of the volume will be fulfilled if it facilitates a deeper understanding of theology in so far as philosophy is concerned.

Why This Book Has Been Written

The reader may begin reading this book with a question in mind. Why another book on a subject addressed by so many learned authors? Like most authors, I sense a need which has not been met by the many works I have examined. That is to say, there are specific interests and issues which I would like to address. This means that I will package and discuss much of the same knowledge which is available in other sources in a different way.

All thought has an autobiographical dimension and is culturally biased. There are givens which are not necessarily negative. Since no neutral thought is possible, it is better to declare from the outset where one is coming from. My pilgrimage of faith has always required serious intellectual reflection. The experience of saving faith as well as a call to the ministry have been for me a mental journey as well as a spiritual pilgrimage. Faith issues for me have always been matters of thought as well as belief. The obvious rejoinder to what I have just said is another question. Granted that some people find the experience of salvation has an intellectual component, why write a book? There are many appropriate responses to this inquiry. I mention only three:

1. Epistemological curiosity is more common than one might think. Many people who seem to be experimenting with different religions and ideas, with no obvious place to stand, need a careful and critical examination of their faith. This is true whether they

acknowledge it or not. There are those who require intellectual honesty with reference to belief, but are fearful of rejection if they dare to ask critical questions about faith or morals. This book is written for those who share what I call "epistemological curiosity" about their faith.

2. Our historical period is filled with ideological confusion. We are beset by the winds of doctrine. But these doctrines are often conveyed by a variety of ideas (historical and contemporary) which need to be recognized, examined and dealt with. Our faith is not secure unless we are prepared to assume this task. This is true of all believers, but especially religious leaders. Religious leaders have the task not only of personal understanding. In addition they are expected to provide knowledge and guidance for others. For example, religious fundamentalism (Christian, Jewish and Islamic) is dominating several modern societies, socially, ethically, economically and politically. A purely pietistic or emotional understanding of faith does not prepare the average believer and citizen to accept or reject these involved realities. Our historical period requires serious thought about what we believe and the faith by which we are prepared to live. Faith has implications for how we relate to others and our role as responsible citizens. This book is written to enable the reader to work through these realities.

3. A holistic faith requires serious thought. I use holistic here with a personal and social meaning. As personal beings we are able to think, will and feel. An integrated personality as well as a healthy religious faith requires coordination of the self around a center of belief. But we are persons-in-community. We are unfulfilled as isolated individuals. We belong in relationship with other persons. We are beings who seek community. Even our relationship to God is incomplete without community with other persons. Any demonstration of religion that exalts God and dehumanizes humans requires the most rigorous intellectual scrutiny. Thus a holistic faith assumes that our faith will be examined carefully and critically. The total self and the network of relationships with the Divine, other humans and all creation, is involved. This holistic understanding of religion requires and deserves the best that our intellects have to offer in the service of faith. This is yet another reason why this book has been written.

Finally, this book has been written with a particular perspective. I will mention two aspects of that perspective at this time.

In the first instance, it is a fact that philosophy has been the means by which theological reflection has taken place. In the study of the history of Christian thought one finds this to be true. Much of Christian theology has been formulated by using Platonism or Aristotelianism as instruments of interpretation of Christian beliefs. When one gets to the modern period, the situation gets more complex because of the progress in natural science and a confluence of cultures and ideas. But the use of philosophy by theologians brings us clearly into the present century. We are on firm ground, therefore, in insisting that we need to know well the history of ideas in order to be knowledgeable about the development and interpretation of Christian doctrines by most major theologians. This is especially true of systematic theologians. To some extent it is also true of biblical theologians, who often rely upon some philosopher for an interpretive apparatus. A good example of the latter was Bultmann's reliance upon Heidegger's fundamental ontology. So I am writing this book on the assumption that the historical development of theology has been dependent upon the history of ideas. It follows that an in-depth examination of the philosophical ideas will enable one better to understand the programs of theology upon which believers and communities of faith depend for the doctrines of the creed.

The second aspect of our perspective takes up the crucial relationship between faith and reason. Which has priority and what is their proper relation? I assume that faith has priority, and reason is a means by which we enrich and enhance our understanding of faith. We love God from the top of our minds as well as from the bottom of our hearts. Faith seeks understanding. The reader is reminded that this conclusion is not original. It was held by Anselm and Augustine. I find it to be a position I can hold with integrity. It is a place to stand, but I am challenged to make it credible in our time, as they did in theirs.

In this chapter I have attempted to introduce this project by engaging the question: why was the book written? I have responded to this question in several ways. I have admitted that all thought is both autobiographical and culturally biased. I discussed epistemological curiosity related to a quest for intellectual integrity of belief. I spoke of the ideological confusion of our historic period and the need for critical thought to work through and sort out a place to stand for our faith. And I discussed faith as a holistic experience. It embraces the whole person as well as the Divine Reality and all human and natural experiences. I then set forth our perspective in two aspects. First I pointed to the fact that philosophy has been an instrument for theological interpretation throughout Christian history. Finally, I indicated that faith and reason are interrelated in our faith-experience, but that we give faith the priority.

Having stated concisely why the book was written, I turn now to the philosophical introduction to theology.

The Theological Use of Philosophy

I could also refer to this section of the introduction as the hermeneutical role of philosophy in the theological task. This may be an odd assumption by one who has been so deeply involved in the advocacy of liberation theological reflection. The justification for this view is not far to seek. Philosophical reflection is a part of my entire vocation as a thinker. I am convinced that having as an avocation the philosophical posture has decisively enriched my personal faith as well as my contribution to theology. Again, I am convinced that philosophy is an essential instrument for all programs in theology, including that of liberation theologians. We are becoming aware of the critical role of other disciplines in the theological task. Sociology, psychology, ethics, anthropology, and even the natural sciences are very useful to theological thinking. But philosophy, even now, is a crucial discipline for interpretation as one develops an interdisciplinary means of interpretation. Finally, I should mention the history of religion as a means of cross-cultural and interreligious theological conversation. In sum, the theological use of philosophy is essential to the theological task.

Throughout Christian history, philosophy has assumed the role of interpretation by which theologians have done their most profound work. In a word, philosophy, having a life of its own, has served theology as a hermeneutical tool. Therefore, a serious encounter with philosophy has been needed to either write or understand major theological texts. This situation remained rather constant up to and through the Middle Ages. Challenges posed by the Renaissance and Enlightenment provide a shift in the role of philosophy in theological discourse. The rise of humanism, rationalism and natural science do not totally eclipse the powerful role of philosophy in theology. Many theologians have continued to make use of the most popular philosophical systems as a means of explicating the Christian faith. This is true in spite of the fact that until now there has been an uneasy truce between philosophy and theology.

What I present at this stage is to be understood as in the nature of generalizations on our subject matter. We shall be looking at these matters in greater detail, but it is essential for me to make my impressions known at the outset.

The more recent challenges have come from the embrace of Naturalism and Positivism by philosophers. But on the side of theology we meet opponents to philosophy. In Protestant theology we find a powerful challenge to the philosophical approach to theology in neo-orthodoxy, under the leadership of Karl Barth. Theology turned anti-intellectual and advocated biblical revelation as the sole source of religious knowledge. This tendency toward anti-intellectualism has now reached its nadir in Fundamentalism, with its infallible Bible and creation-science.

A great deal of philosophical activity goes on even when there is an attempt by philosophers to deny faith, or by theologians to deny critical thinking. The reasons for the persistence of philosophy are at least twofold: 1. critical thinking is an inherent part of human personality; 2. philosophical and theological history are so entangled that anti-intellectual theologians must find reasons against reason to establish an opposing position. For example, both Kierkegaard and Barth use philosophy against philosophy. Conversely, philosophers who would denounce the logic of faith must face formidable thinkers in the ranks of theologians. It is interesting to note the intensity of anti-faith reflection by many Logical Positivists.

The recent conflict between philosophy and theology is most evident in universities on behalf of philosophers, and in seminaries on the side of theologians. Many colleges and universities have downgraded the study of religion and theology in the name of science and/or analytical philosophy. On the other hand, more conservative seminaries have ceased to take philosophy seriously any more. This has been done in the name of biblicism and the desire to purify the faith. In some intellectual centers, philosophers of the left became indifferent or totally hostile to religion as a relic of the pre-scientific age. Theologians on the right tend to shun philosophy as useless and even dangerous speculation. The present climate is indeed confused. In my judgment the situation calls for serious critical and constructive philosophical analysis and reflection on religion and theology.

The insights of Professor George Thomas are decisive for my purpose, and I use here an extensive quotation from a major work:

> Almost from the beginning of Western philosophy in ancient Greece, the criticism of popular religion has been one of the major sources of development in religious thought. As Xenophanes poured scorn upon the anthropomorphism of early Greek religion, Plato attacked the myths of the popular polytheism which pictured the gods as causing evil as well as good in the lives of men. In Jewish and Christian thought, also, philosophers have insisted upon the use of reason to challenge arbitrary and unworthy beliefs about God and His relation to man. Thus, philosophy has been a powerful force in the criticism of irrational elements in the great religions of the West.[3]

> Philosophy is useful in helping religion to achieve unity in beliefs and in relating them to beliefs derived from other sources. The origin of religion is in experience, intuition and imagination rather than in logical thinking. Hence religious beliefs are often inconsistent and in need of coherence through reason. We need to be able to clarify beliefs according to their priority. For example, the Christian belief in eternal life needs to be distinguished from mythological images of the afterlife. Philosophy can assist religion by purging it of internal inconsistencies and naive interpretations. In addition, philosophy can assist in the process of relating religious beliefs to knowledge derived from social science, natural science, the humanities and the arts, thus making clearer the implications of religious beliefs for human life.[4]

> A common ground for religion and philosophy is the articulation of a world-view.[5] This makes philosophy important to religious belief as the means by which concepts and principles for interpretation are available. The language of religion is usually concrete, while the language of philosophy is mainly abstract. It is, however, necessary for religious beliefs to be expressed in abstract or conceptual terms for the purpose of clarifying and communicating them. Human beings are rational beings who seek to understand their religious beliefs. We assume that this potentially is and should be so. We are also social beings who wish to share with others as effectively as possible. This is why religious beliefs need to come to terms with the philosophy of each age if it is not to be divorced from the thought of the time.

I use here a case from Judaism. This is most appropriate, since the interrelation between Christianity and Judaism has been very close in the West. I shall refer to three Jewish thinkers, Philo, Maimonides and Buber, representing three historic periods. Philo used Platonism; Maimonides, Aristotelianism; and Buber, Existentialism. All were devout Jewish theologians who expressed their faith through the problems and needs of a particular age. Since humans need a world-view to forge meaning out of life, every age forces competing world-views upon us. This situation demands rigorous philosophical thought to purge unworthy beliefs out of our minds, through criticism and the quest for consistency in beliefs. We need a world-view which is compatible with faith and at the same time worthy of the best use of reason.

Philosophy has a *critical* task in reference to the claims of religious beliefs to truth. If the description of philosophy by Plato is taken seriously, this is quite obvious. Plato defined philosophy as reflection upon "all time and all existence." If, then, philosophy is to do justice to all fields of human experience and thought, there is surely the task of clarifying the fundamental concepts and assertions of religion. Religion claims to provide insight into the nature of reality and life as a whole. The claims of religion are too comprehensive and crucial not to be brought under the scrutiny of reason.[6] It is important to be able to use philosophy and vital religious faith. It is helpful to be reminded of Pascal's distinction between the *knowledge* of God and the *love* of God.[7]

Again, philosophy has a *constructive* task as regards religious belief. Whether or not this function is realized depends upon the manner in which philosophy is used. This in turn may relate either to the attitude of a particular philosopher to religious faith or to the employment of a philosopher's ideas by a theologian. As a theologian, I assume that the benefits of encounter between philosophy and theology are mutually enriching. They are both impoverished if a respectful encounter is not achieved.

The task of philosophy is not to refute religious beliefs outright or to deny the validity of their possibility, as some logical positivists and analytical philosophers have done. I am aware that some philosophers dedicate themselves to the discovery of new truths which are seen to compete with or even replace time-honored religious beliefs. Thus their contribution is *negative* or *destructive*. My interest is in the *constructive* function of philosophy for a profound understanding of religious beliefs.

The task of philosophy is not to construct a new religion based on reason alone which will supersede the religions of the past and present. It is to formulate clearly the beliefs of religious persons and to develop these and their implications for an understanding of the world and human life, and to inquire critically into their truth and value. It is to reflect upon the religious ideas and beliefs which have actually existed, and to evaluate their claims. This view does not preclude that a philosopher may also be a theologian. There are many philosophical theologians in the history of Western thought. Among these are Augustine, Aquinas and Kierkegaard. The hesitation of some religious persons to think philosophically is due to the assumption that the role of philosophy is to give reasons why religious beliefs should be rejected. My discussion is clearly directed in the opposite direction of a constructive use of philosophy in the interpretation of religious beliefs.

In this encounter the philosopher's role is secondary. The philosopher has an interpretative role. Religious beliefs have existed throughout all known history. Their origin is even prehistorical. They represent living experience and a way of life for millions of people. If the founders of religions like prophets, mystics and ordinary religious persons had not expressed their religious experiences and beliefs in intelligible language, the philosopher would not have religious data to excite his/her interest and claim attention. Philosophy functions as an instrument for religious understanding once it assumes the reality and validity of religion as an experience to be interpreted, criticized and evaluated. The constructive task of philosophy may be to formulate precise questions as well as to reflect profoundly upon religious answers to significant questions. Philosophers usually provide a theory of knowledge or metaphysics as a means to an end. This study is about this important task.

II

The Early Greek Experience

The Meaning and History of Philosophy

"Striving after wisdom," or the love of wisdom as viewed by persons like Socrates, Plato and Aristotle, is the subject-matter of this section. The Germans refer to philosophy as *Wissenschaft*. Philosophy is *science* in which individual realms of existence are to be investigated and known. This has a greater range than the English or French meaning of *science*. For instance, the meaning of *Wissenschaft* as *science* or *scientific* is broader than natural science.

The above was the first definition of philosophy. But, a second meaning was also associated with philosophy very early. It arose in Greece at a time when naive religions and ethical consciousness were in a state of disintegration. This made questions concerning the human vocation more important for investigation. Instruction in the right conduct of life became an essential aim, shaping the main content of philosophy or science. Thus philosophy received the *practical meaning* of the art of life, based upon scientific principles. This latter meaning was introduced by the Sophists and Socrates.

Pre-Socratic Philosophy. Greek religions had dominated the scene prior to Thales (born 624 B.C.). But with Thales the problem of *substance* was pushed to the center of concern.

While most ancient people seemed to rest in their mythological stage, the Greeks did not. They moved early to a philosophical stage. (Greek thought evolved from simple mythological notions to complex and comprehensive systems of thought.)

The reasons for this development may be traceable to certain social and environmental factors. These are obviously not the total explanation for the Greek philosophical genius. We note, however, some of these factors.

Greece is a mountain peninsula. This territory possesses characteristics favorable to the development of a strong active race. It possesses many harbors, attractive for navigation and commerce. There were outlets for emigration over the islands to other lands. Greek colonies were established in a chain from the mainland to the coasts of Asia Minor to such destinations as Egypt, Sicily and Southern Italy. These social, cultural and economic benefits produced a type of cosmopolitan attitude early in history. They stimulated both intellect and will, quickened the spirit of criticism and reflection, developed unique personalities and made progress along the lines of human thought and will possible.

The Greeks were, however, naturally endowed with a keen and quick intelligence, a burning thirst for knowledge, a fine sense of beauty and practical energy and ambition. These attributes led to rapid progress in politics, religion, morals, literature and philosophy.

Politics evolved from a patriarchal monarchy through aristocracy to democracy. The society described by Homer in his epics was a caste society under a patriarchal monarchy. The acquisition of wealth and culture by the few led to an aristocratic form of government, often ending in oligarchies. But a citizen class (the *Demos*) arose and began to dispute the leadership of the privileged class. This transition from aristocracy to democracy took place during the seventh and sixth centuries B.C.

Literature often took the form of protest. It represented the opposition to the traditional outlook and indicated the demand for reform. A type of enlightenment expressed itself through literary protest.

The history of Greek literature before the sixth century B.C. reveals the development of a spirit of reflection and criticism similar to that expressing itself in political life. Poets became more pessimistic, more critical and reflective. Homer moved from a preoccupation with cheerfulness and objectivity to moral reflections on human behavior, the misery and transitoriness of life and the evils of injustice.

Hesiod sounded loudly the note of criticism and pessimism. His *Works and Days* is a moral handbook in which he attacks the foibles of the age and offers moral advice based upon the virtues of traditional family life. This is true of other poets, even fable writers.

All around, individuals arose who analyzed and criticized life. They pondered its meaning and were no longer content to accept concepts and ideals blindly. This spirit of free inquiry culminated in a philosophical study of human conduct.

The Religious Origins of Greek Philosophy. The relation between religion and philosophy in Greece was both intimate and complicated. Historical evidence is inclusive. Would-be authorities are not in agreement on salient points.

Greek religion had two aspects: (1.) The religion of the gods of Olympus, made famous by the epics of Homer. These gods were in some sense supernatural, but with human passions and greatly involved in human affairs. These anthropomorphic figures evolved over a long period and culminated in the fifth and fourth centuries B.C. This development was closely related to the emergence of philosophy (2.) The other aspect of Greek religion is associated with mystery cults.

In Greece religion, art and philosophy are closely related and often cross-fertilize each other. For instance, in Homer, the god Zeus is, like other gods, subject to fate. But later in the dramas of Aeschylus, fate itself came to be identified with the supreme will of Zeus. The religion of the Olympian gods influenced philosophy, only to be influenced in turn by conceptions developed independently in philosophy as well as a later religious revival in the sixth century B.C. These religious influences are especially evident in Pythagoras, Parmenides, Heraclitus, Socrates, Plato and Aristotle — down to the fourth century B.C.

Aristotle speaks of Hesiod as an early Greek theologian. Aristotle, however, contrasts the method of theologians with the first philosophers. He observed that these early writers in their theologies promulgated doctrines and attempted explanations in mythical form, while the first philosophers used methods of strict proof. The point to be made is that these early theogonies prepared the way for a more systematic philosophical period.

Philosophy of Nature[2]

Philosophy before the Sophists was focused upon nature. The earliest philosophical school was established in the colony of Miletus by Thales (b. 624 B.C.). He was a statesman, mathematician, astronomer, as well as the first philosopher. He left no written work. Our knowledge of his teachings is secondary.

Thales is the acknowledged founder of a school which explored the problem of substance. The Milesian philosophers asked the question: what is the original stuff of which the world is composed? These thinkers turned away from mythical beings towards knowledge based on experience—that which is given through the senses. The starting point of their philosophizing was "the things that exist." This referred to everything accessible to sense perception. Their aim was to determine the nature, or *physis*, of things. The word originally pertained to an act of growth, and to the source from which growth springs. Thus the nature of a thing refers to its one underlying, living, and generative reality. Reality is conceived of in terms of growth and generation.

Thales declared water to be the original stuff. He perhaps based his conclusion on the fact that nourishment, heat, and seed which are essential to life contain moisture. He viewed nature as being alive, as moving, acting and changing. His conclusions were three in number: 1. all things are full of gods; 2. the earth is a flat disc floating on water; and 3. water is the material cause of all things.

Thales was followed by Anaximander. The latter was a younger person and perhaps a student of Thales, though he is sometimes referred to as an associate. Anaximander was engaged in practical scientific pursuits. He is credited with constructing a map for sailors on the Black Sea. He was actively involved in politics as well.

Anaximander was born in Miletus in 611 B.C. He was interested in astronomy, geography and cosmology. He made maps of the earth and heavens and introduced the sundial in Greece. His work entitled *On Nature* is said to be the first philosophical book in Greece as well as the first prose work in Greek.

He reasoned in this manner. The essence or principle of things is the Boundless or Infinite—an eternal imperishable substance out of which all things return. He meant a boundless space-filling, animate mass. Unfortunately, he is not precise in his meaning. Several views have resulted. Examples are these: 1. the Boundless is a mixture from which all things arise by separation; 2. it is indefinite, indeterminate and qualitatively undifferentiated matter (cf. Aristotle's "indeterminate potential matter"), or; 3. it is something intermediate between the observable elements—i.e., water, air and fire. He reasons that the Boundless must be infinite, indefinite in extent—otherwise it would be consumed in the creation of things.

Anaximander's thought is based upon his reaction to Thales. But, for him, the element water is derivative rather than the primary principle of existence. He goes beyond Thales in attempting to describe the stages of the process of becoming and he suggests somewhat the indestructibility of matter. And yet his reluctance to ascribe quality to what he called the Boundless leaves his thought more abstract than that of Thales. Thales was looking for a concrete, sense-perceived substance. The Boundless does not reach that degree of concreteness.

From this mass, different substances are separated in consequence of its eternal motion: first the hot and then the cold, the hot surrounding the cold as a sphere of flame. The heat of the flame turns the cold into moisture, and then into air, which expands and breaks up the sphere of fire into wheel-shaped rings. The rings have openings like holes of a flute, through which fire streams, and these are the heavenly bodies, which the air, surrounding them, forces to move around the earth. The sun is the most remote body in the heavens; next comes the moon, and then the fixed stars and planets. The earth is the center of this system—it is a cylindrical body. Anaximander seems to anticipate some of the assumptions of modern astronomy, by insisting that the earth is unsupported by anything but is held in equilibrium by other bodies.

Everything arose out of the moist element, but later some of these creatures inhabit a new, drier surrounding. Humans, like all animals, began as a fish. Everything must return again to the primal mass whence it sprang, only to be produced anew *ad infinitum*. He posits a doctrine of cyclical recurrence: innumerable worlds succeed one another in time, but are not co-existent. This cosmological hypothesis resembles recent cyclical theories of history.

The Boundless of Anaximander, as we have seen, is not as concrete as water, the substance of Thales. It is not, however, viewed as abstract infinitude. It is described as a concrete indeterminate substance or as an infinite concrete mass. Even so, the Boundless differs from the particular things observable by the senses. Anaximander's view represents a measure of philosophical sophistication beyond Thales.

The final person in the ranks of these early Milesian philosophers of nature was Anaximenes (588–524 B.C.). He was another citizen of Miletus and a pupil of Anaximander. He wrote a prose work in the Ionic dialect. Unfortunately, only a small fragment is left.

Anaximenes took air, vapor or mist as his original substance. He wanted a dry and cold element which is between fire and water. Air is said to be the principle of life in our bodies. Without breath the organism dies. Air or breath is the life-giving element in humans— it is likewise the principle of the universe. He asserted that the world breathes. A human soul, as air, holds one together, so breath or air surrounds or sustains the whole world. The cosmic air is animate and extends infinitely through space.

The main advance of Anaximenes over Thales and Anaximander appears to be his doctrine of rarefaction and condensation, as he seeks to explain the emergence of the observable elements from the primary substance. When air is rarefied it becomes fire; condensed, it becomes wind, cloud, water, earth and stone. *Condensation* and *rarefaction* are quantitative notions—the former an increase, the latter a decrease in the amount of matter occupying a given space.

The theory of Anaximenes moves in the direction of the reduction of qualitative difference to quantitative terms—i.e. the "atomism" of Democritus. Another way of stating the case is to assert that Anaximenes sought to effect the reduction of all change to motion. All changes are said to be produced by motion, and motion is eternal. Through this crucial insight, Anaximenes appears to anticipate Aristotle as well as subsequent natural scientific philosophy and history.

Religious Revival

A religious revival took place toward the end of the sixth century B.C. In contrast to the Olympian stage of Greek religion, this latter movement was based among common people. Even when Homer wrote, ordinary people venerated local gods which represented the primeval forces related to their struggle with the soil. These local gods often enjoyed a greater ritualistic importance than the gods associated with the aristocratic myths. In popular religiosity, the gods often retained the names and character of the Olympian gods, thus reflecting the seminal influence of the former movement upon the popular religion.

The local gods came into their own during the sixth century. Their importance grew as the masses got involved in political matters. This new religiosity was a sign of the growing power of the wider populace. A form of worship familiar to the countryside made its way into the cities, when masses of countryfolk were displaced as a result of economic changes. The worship of these gods was often encouraged as a means of political control. This was a common demagogic measure employed by tyrants who ruled at the time.

Dionysus, a Thracian god of barbaric aspect, was welcomed by the priesthood of *Apollo*. *Demeter*, a goddess of the countryside, was readily assimilated by the Olympian cluster of gods. The worship of *Dionysus* was central to the cult practice of this religious renaissance. Like *Eleusis*, *Dionysus* was associated with the revivification of the earth in the spring, symbolized by the resurrection after death, or return after disappearance, of the gods.

Again, *Dionysus* was worshipped as the god of the vine and *Demeter* as the goddess of grain. Cults like those associated with *Dionysus* were to be found from place to place. These had as their center rituals called mysteries through which the initiated were thought to achieve unity with the gods.

Worship was both private and public (even official), involving what became known as "sacraments." These esoteric rites as expressed in public worship influenced Greek drama. These Dionysian cults were modified by religion associated with *Orpheus*, a mythical Thracian singer who charmed with his lyre not only humans and beasts but also gods.

Orpheus, by the sweetness of his music, persuaded the Queen of Hades to return his beloved to him. He was, however, finally torn to pieces by maenads, the raving women voteries of the god *Dionysus* with whom he is associated. *Orpheus* thus became identified with the deity, who, in an Orphic version of Dionysaic myth, is also torn to pieces before his rebirth.

The Orphic influence is less barbaric than its Dionysiac background. It contains an ethical element in its striving for immortality through identification with the god, Dionysus. For example, rites which were formerly sexually explicit now became ascetic. As the mystery rites moved into civic life, much of their barbaric character was removed. The Orphic influence is a refinement of this religious revival. The figure of Orpheus is often referred to as a tamed and clothed Dionysus.

Thus many of the influences of the sixth-century religious revival may be traced in philosophy through Orphic characteristics. We note first the doctrine of the soul as manifest in the Pythagorean brotherhood. The Orphic cults believed in the transmigration of the soul, which was thought to be immortal, and to have undergone a primal fall from a perfect state. In successive re-incarnation the soul seeks to return to that blessed status.

This ethical concern modified the emphasis in the Dionysiac cult on the renewal of the earth. Through its identification of the soul principle with the mind in the Pythagoreans, and through similar tendencies in the later Anaxagoras, the way was paved for the views held by Plato and Aristotle about the rational character of the divine principle and its association with the human soul.

This religious revival does not imply philosophy in a proper sense, but it does afford a suitable background for the development of religiously oriented thought. Thus Pythagoras, Parmenides and Heraclitus, among others, reflect the congruence with the religious life of the times without indicating its direct influence. These philosophers express themselves with a fervor reminiscent of the contemporary poets—i.e. Aeschylus and Pindar. It is to be observed that sixth-century religious life has its highest expression in such philosophers and poets, rather than in the mystery cults.

We recall that the Milesian philosophers seized upon natural scientific knowledge based upon sense experience. Though they had some concern with the Divine, it was not primary. Their first interest was in the material and space-filling aspects or things presented in sense perception. Pythagoras, Parmenides and Heraclitus preserve the intellectualism of the Milesians, but they place greater emphasis on the apprehension of the Divine as such.

Early Religio-Ethical Philosophy

The founder of the Pythagorean School was Pythagoras. He was known as a traveller and this is reflected in his ideas. He was born in Samos between 580 and 570 B.C. He emigrated to Greek colonies in southern Italy about 529 B.C. Pythagoras opposed tyrannical rule. He settled in Crotona where he founded an association for ethical, political and religious purposes.

Pythagoras desired to develop political virtues—among his followers to teach them to act for the good of the state. They were to subordinate themselves for the good of the community. Individuals should gain self-control in order to subdue passions, harmonize the soul, have respect for authority and recognize the proper place of teachers, elders and the state. The Pythagorean Brotherhood was established as a practical training school for citizenship and as a test of the teachings of Pythagoras.

Pythagoras exalted the virtues of friendship and self-examination. His community was a place where members became a family. They ate together, dressed alike, studied arts and crafts, music, medicine and mathematics. Pythagoras appealed to the upper classes, but with religious foundations in the religious revivalism of the mystery cults. The aim of religious worship and ritual was to purify life. It was assumed that the future destiny of the soul was dependent on human conduct during earthly life.

Pythagoras was to have wide influence on several fields of knowledge. Here we will discuss his representative contribution to number-theory, astronomy and ethics.

The Pythagoreans were impressed with forms and relation in the world. They found measure, order, proportion, and uniform recurrence as expressions of numbers. They asserted that without number, there can be no such relations and uniformities. Number must, therefore, be the basis of everything. Numbers are not the stuff or substance in the Milesian sense. Numbers constitute their formal or rational structure. Things were said to be the copies of imitations of numbers. The later distinction between matter and form in classical Greek philosophy was anticipated in the Pythagorean distinction between numbers and things.

For this group of thinkers, numbers were to be compared with the causal laws of nature — they were viewed as the causes of all that happened. For instance, there is a relation between the length of the string and the pitch of the tone in music. Number, which is only a symbol and expression of the relation, was assumed to be the *cause* of the relation. Thus for the Pythagoreans number is the foundational principle and ground of all things.

It follows that whatever is true of number is also true of things, since number is their essence. The Pythagoreans reasoned from peculiarities discoverable in numbers to the attributes in the universe at large. Numbers are odd and even — finite and infinite, limited and unlimited; these constitute the essence of number and reality. Nature is a union of opposites, of odd and even. They set up a table of ten opposites, as follows:

a   limited and unlimited
b   odd and even
c   one and many
d   right and left
e   male and female
f   rest and motion
g   straight and crooked

h   light and darkness
i   good and bad
j   square and rectangle.

The Pythagorean doctrine of dualism had its roots in the thought of Anaximander and Anaximenes. The Pythagoreans regarded the unlimited as prior to the limited. That is to say, individual things arise through the limitation of the unlimited space by the imposition of forms on space.

The material world is also numerical, being based on the unit. The point is one, the line two, the figure three, the solid four, and so on. Lines and surfaces of bodies were conceived as entities having an independent existence.

The Pythagoreans assumed that there can be no bodies without lines and surfaces can be thought without bodies. The special forms are the causes of the bodies, since the forms can be expressed by numbers—numbers are the ultimate causes. Arithmetical distinctions are thus carried into the physical world. They were led to affirm an unlimited space or void which contracts with the limited bodies in space.

The influence of Pythagorean number mysticism on physics and astronomy is great. The theories of Kepler display marked influences from this tradition. What has been lasting is the attempt to discover the order and lawfulness in things and to formulate this order in abstract conceptual terms of numbers or numerical relations. This insistence upon a conception of a mathematically expressible natural law is at the core of modern science.

The attention which the Pythagoreans gave to astronomy should be briefly mentioned. Several members of the school became astronomers. They made contributions to the astronomical theories leading to the heliocentric theory of the universe as advocated by Aristarchus of Samos about 280 B.C. According to T. S. Kuhn, if the work of Aristarchus had been taken seriously, the heliocentric astronomy might have developed eighteen centuries earlier than it did.[3]

Finally, ethics is also derived from Pythagorean number-mysticism. Non-material things were said to have their parallels in material things: love, friendship, justice, virtue and health are based on numbers. Love and friendship are expressed by the number eight, because they represent harmony and the octave indicates harmony. Pythagoras is said to have likened life to a public game in which three classes of people are distinguishable: the buyers and sellers (vendors) who have no interest in the game but only seek profit; the participants who are seeking praise and honor; and the observers whose aim is neither gain nor honor but wisdom.

The Pythagorean movement took a popular turn which began to influence ordinary people. The Brotherhood ran into conflict with the established political order. Pythagoras was exiled and forced to seek refuge in Metapontum, where he died in 500 B.C. His movement was scattered, but his doctrines influenced Greek thought and life for centuries. He set in motion ideas, the fruits of which are still with us.

Being and Becoming

The Ionian physicist-philosophers explored the substantial nature of things. The Pythagoreans were obsessed with quantitative relations, order, harmony and number. The next problem was change or becoming. Change had been implicit in the explanations of the early philosophers, but it did not become a focal point. The problem presented itself with such force that a group of philosophers emerged who pushed the problem of becoming to the center of their systems of thought.

This is what Heraclitus did. He was deeply impressed with the fact of change in the world and insisted that change constitutes the very life of the universe. Nothing was believed to be really permanent. Heraclitus asserted that permanence is an illusion. Things may appear to remain constant, but they are actually in an endless process of becoming — a state of incessant flux.

Heraclitus (535–475 B.C.) was born in Ephesus, the son of a noble family. He was an aristocrat with a contempt for democracy. Heraclitus was serious and pessimistic. He was said to be dogmatic, proud and inclined toward extreme criticism of others. His style was obscure and difficult. And yet he was a forceful writer, full of wise and original sayings. Several works are ascribed to him, but only fragments remain. An example is the work titled *On Nature*, which is divided into three parts: physical, ethical and political.

Heraclitus is known by his famous statement: "One cannot step twice into the same river; for other and yet other waters are ever flowing on." Against the background of this assumption, he takes up several sub-topics.

First, we consider the relation between fire and the universal flux.

Heraclitus wanted for his first principle something which expresses the notion of incessant activity. The most restless and mobile substance he knew was fire. It never rests—it is ever-living. Fire is often called vapor or breath. Breath is the vital principle in the organism and the essence of the soul. Heraclitus does not enter into a constructive statement on whether fire is a concrete physical substance or a symbol for ceaseless activity or process. What he wanted was a principle that undergoes continual qualitative transformation. Fire satisfied this demand. Fire for Heraclitus was not an abiding substratum; it was constantly being transformed into other things.

Second, we examine his insights on opposites and their union. Primal unity itself is a constant motion and change; its creation is destruction, its destruction creation. When it passes into something else (e.g. from fire to water) the fire is lost in a new form of existence. Everything is changed into its opposite and everything is a union of opposite qualities. There are no persistent qualities, hence nothing remains permanent by virtue of its qualities. Everything both is and is not. The universal process is a transition from one condition to its opposite and, in this sense, everything unites opposites within itself. Such opposition alone makes the world possible. Harmony in music, for example, results from the combination of high notes and low notes, i.e. from the union of opposites.

Harmony is the union of opposites and at the same time it is the law governing the process of change. The process and its law are identical. Through his stress on becoming, Heraclitus anticipates *Hegelian* evolutionary and process thought. He resembles Hegel in this regard as well as in his emphasis upon the union of opposites.

Third, he relates harmony and reason. According to Heraclitus, the cosmic process is governed by law. There is a pre-established principle of harmony in the universe, indifferent to human or divine wills. The order of things is the work of Fate or Justice. Change, therefore, is a matter of necessity. In the midst of all change and contradiction, the only thing that persists or remains the same is the inexorable law that underlies all movement, change and opposition; it is the reason in things, the *logos*. This is a rational principle—it is alive and endowed with reason. We are not clear whether Heraclitus meant by *logos* "a conscious intelligence" or "an impersonal rationality." His thought, however, does influence the important *logos* tradition in philosophy which is so significant in Jewish, Christian and Islamic theology.

Fourth, we assess succinctly his understanding of psychology and ethics. The human soul, according to Heraclitus, is part of the universal fire and nourished by it. We breathe and receive it through our senses. The driest and warmest soul is the best soul, most like the cosmic fire-soul. Sense knowledge is inferior to reason; the eyes and ears are poor witnesses. Perception without reflection does not reveal the hidden truth, which is discernible by reason. The controlling element in man is the soul which is akin to divine reasoning. Humans in their moral conduct must subordinate themselves to the universal reason. To be ethical is to live a rational life, to obey the dictates of reason, which is the same everywhere. Morality means respect for law, self-discipline, control of passions. To be moral is to govern oneself by rational principles. Because of his ethical relativism Heraclitus resembles Epicurus. And yet in his rationalism and emphasis upon natural law he anticipates the Stoics. It is said that he tended toward a moral aristocracy with contempt for the masses in ethics and religiosity. In this regard he points to the philosopher-king class of Plato.

On the other side of the spectrum, the Eleatics were preoccupied with permanence. As the name implies, this group of thinkers emerged from a town known as Elea. They held that change is unthinkable since the principle of things must be unmoved. Elea was in southern Italy, and the most important philosophers of this school were Parmenides, Xenophanes and Zeno.

Xenophanes (570–480 B.C.) was a poet, skeptic and theologian who emigrated to Colophon in Asia Minor into Southern Italy. He was a skeptic who lived the life of a migrant. As a satirical poet, Xenophanes criticized Greek manners and beliefs. He opposed vigorously prevailing polytheism. He was a skeptic in temper of mind and attitude rather than a systematic philosopher.

It may be said that Xenophanes was more a speculative theologian than a philosopher. He was under the influence of the popular religious movement of the sixth century B.C. He was preoccupied with the unity and unchangeableness of God. He opposed polytheism and was certain that God is unlike mortals in body and mind. God abides in one place and does not move. God is eternal—without beginning or end. There is nothing beside God (the unlimited), but as a sphere, God is limited, a perfect form rather than formless infinite. God is immoveable as a whole, for motion is inconsistent with the unity of being. There is, however, motion or change in God's parts.

Xenophanes was a pantheist. He conceived God as the eternal principle of the universe, as the One and All in which everything is. God, in other words, is the world; God is not pure spirit, but all of animate nature. Xenophanes reduced God to the level of the forces of nature rather than elevating the world to the level of the divine. He was unable to overcome the incompatibility between God and the world, thus leaving a serious challenge for his successors. He accepted the hylozoism of the early Greeks by holding that the world is animate. If he believed in the gods of polytheism at all, they were mere natural phenomena. God was for him a divinity animating the world. It is obvious that in his pursuit of the problem of God, Xenophanes raised important questions for both philosophers and theologians.

Parmenides was the metaphysician of the Eleatic school. He developed its ontology. He challenged Heraclitus forthrightly on the issue of change. He boldly defended permanency. According to Parmenides, the theory of Heraclitus regarding the principle of existence as incessant change is absurd. Heraclitus seemed to say that something is and is not at the same time. Again, Heraclitus appeared to argue that something can become nothing. If being has *become*, it must have come either from non-being or from being. If from non-being, it has come from nothing. This is impossible. On the other hand, if it has come from being, then being has come from itself—it is identical with itself and, therefore, has always been.

According to Parmenides, being comes from being. A thing cannot become something else. Whatever is has always been and always will be and remains the same. Hence there can be only one eternal, underived, unchangeable being. Being is continuous and indivisible, there is no break in it. There is no non-being since there is no empty space for it to occupy.

Again, being and thought are one; for whatever cannot be thought, cannot be; and what cannot be (i.e. non being) cannot be thought. Thought and being are identical; for what can be thought must also be. Reality is endowed with mind. Logical thought compels us to conceive of the world as a unity, as unchangeable and immoveable. Sense perception, on the contrary, reveals to us the world of plurality and change; this is a world of appearance and opinion. In many ways this argument resembles the ontological argument for the existence of God presented by Anselm.

Finally, we notice that Parmenides reasons from language to reality. He draws metaphysical conclusions from language. His challenge presents itself to recent philosophers of language. Bertrand Russell, for example, is one of the modern philosophers who has noted the challenge of Parmenides. Parmenides' many influences upon the history of philosophy as well as theology deserve much attention.

Zeno made a bold attempt to establish his belief in permanence as a dialectician. His proofs of permanence as the principle of existence are known as paradoxes of motion. They are the following.

Zeno attempts to demonstrate the impossibility of moving from a position to a goal because of the necessity of passing through the numerous points between the starting point and the goal.

First, he presents the paradox of Achilles and the tortoise. Achilles moves from his starting point to the tortoise's initial starting point. Meanwhile, the tortoise has moved a certain distance beyond, and the same holds for all subsequent intervals.

Second, Zeno presents his paradox of the moving arrow. He attempts to demonstrate that the arrow moving to its target is in any instant in a definite position in space. In other words, the arrow always remains at rest or zero motion and no summation of zeroes can yield motion.

Third, Zeno appeals to the relativity of observed motions. The conflicting testimony of the senses, depending upon whether a moving object is observed from a position at rest or in motion at various speeds, undermines the very possibility of motion as such.

Zeno's arguments rest upon a questionable assumption, viz., that space and time consist of discrete instants and points respectively. His paradoxes can be resolved only in the context of mathematical, physical or philosophical theories of the continuum of reality.

Melissus of Samos also embraced the Eleatic doctrine. Melissus agreed with Parmenides that being is one. Being cannot be originated. Being cannot come from non-being. Being is infinite and eternal. He disagrees with Parmenides, however, in his doctrine of the spatial infinite (or unlimited space). This placed Melissus not only against the assertion of finite space by Parmenides, but over against the general tendency of Greek thought to repudiate the infinite as meaningless or unthinkable. Since there is no empty space or non-being, motion, which requires space, is impossible. There is neither separation of combination—there is neither multiplicity or motion—hence, no change. The senses merely deceive us in presenting motion and change.

According to the Eleatic school nothing can arise or disappear.

nothing can change into anything else, no quality can become another quality; for that would mean the disappearance of a quality on the one hand, and the creation of a quality on the other. Reality is conceived as being permanent and unchangeable. Change is a fiction for which the senses are responsible. But the school's efforts lack the content that make them convincing. They do raise issues that require serious reflection. Things seems to persist as well as change. Philosophy could not leave the matter thus. The static and dynamic views of relating reality had to be addressed.

Qualitative and Quantitative Theories of Reality

The discussion on how things change and how they remain constant is pursued by Empedocles and Anaxagoras on the qualitative side. It is discussed on the quantitative side by Leucippus and Democritus.

Empedocles was born in Sicily in 495 B.C. He was son of a wealthy and political family and was a political leader himself. He is said to have declined a kingship. He was a religious teacher, a physician, a poet and a philosopher. Two poems — *On Nature* and *Purifications* — are ascribed to him. He died an exile in the Peloponnese in 435 B.C.

The union and division of elements was his main question. Empedocles insists that there is only mingling and separation — there is neither origin or decay.

According to Empedocles there are four elements which are the "root of things:" air, earth, fire and water. Each element has a specific nature. These elements are underived, unchangeable and indestructable. Bodies are destroyed by their coming together or destroyed by their dissolution. The influence of one body on another is explained by passing of effusions from one into the pores of the other.

This process has its primal explanation in two mythical forces, Love and Strife (Hate), in addition to the union and separation of the four elements. Love and Hate are the two motive forces, attraction and repulsion. These may exist side by side, first causing bodies to be formed and later causing them to be destroyed.

When Love has the upper hand there is union. When Strife dominates, there is separation. When there is an intermediate stage, there is an admixture of Love and Hate. The cosmos and human life are explained by this same process of mingling and separation. Like is known of like. Humans are composed of the four elements. For Empedocles the heart was the seat of intelligence. He believed that psychic life inhabited all things and in them resided the power of thought. His religious thought included the fall of humans, the transmigration of souls — revealing Orphic influence.

In sum, Empedocles argued that there is no such thing as absolute change. But there is relative change which results from the impact of the two mythical motive forces on four elements, earth, air, fire and water. This process is one of union and separation. It continues indefinitely.

Anaxagoras joined Empedocles in the attempt to explain the phenomenon of change. Anaxagoras was born in 500 B.C. and died in Asia Minor in 428 B.C. He was an Athenian and friend of Pericles. He desired to make Athens the intellectual and political center of Greece. Being accused of atheism, Anaxagoras was forced to leave Athens after thirty years and settled in Lampsacus, where he died. He was a noted mathematician, astronomer and philosopher. His known work was entitled *On Nature*. Fragments of this work remain available.

Anaxagoras accepted the Eleatic notion that no quality can become another quality, that reality must be permanent and unchangeable in its fundamental essence. He refused, however, to reject the fact of change. He supports the argument of Empedocles that change takes place in relative terms only.

According to Anaxagoras, the mingling and separation of elements does take place. He observed, however, that the elements of air, earth, fire and water are too few to explain the richness and fullness of qualities in the world. There must be an infinite number of substances of specific quality. The elements suggested by Empedocles were viewed as mixtures of substances and not elements in their own right; they were more complex, and composed of a multitude of extremely small particles of matter of all kinds.

The world is made up of particles composing this mass. Anaxagoras asked how the seeds were separated from the chaos in which they lay scattered, and then united into a cosmos or world-order. He argued that the seeds were not endowed with life, nor were they moved by Love or Hate as Empedocles had assumed. Anaxagoras believed that the process took place through a rapid whirling motion which brought the particles together. This activity continued to spread until the original chaotic mixture was completely disentangled.

According to Anaxagoras, there is another cause. Behind this complex world-process, he posited an intelligent principle, a *Mind* or *Nous*, a world-ordering spirit. Anaxagoras understood this principle to be a simple and homogeneous substance. It is distinct from other elements or seeds—it has power over matter.

The *Nous* principle is a unique and valuable contribution and deserves further explication. It is a spontaneous active being, the free source of all movement and life in the world. It knows all things, past, present and future. The *Nous* arranges all things and is the cause of all things. It rules over all that has life and is teleological or purposeful. Anaxagoras asserted that there is only one world. There are no successive or contemporaneous worlds. This ordering mind forms only the one unique and most perfect world.

We meet in Greek philosophy for the first time an attempt to link teleology and intelligence with the uniqueness and perfection of the world-order. It follows that if the world-scheme is the product of purposive mind, there can be no cyclical recurrence such as Empedocles had asserted.

While in Anaxagoras, mind appears to be a distinct principle, we are not clear as to whether it is pure spirit or a form of matter or mixture. There is the possibility of a dualism not yet defined. Mind is, however, the force that initiated the world-process: it is present in the world in organic forms, and wherever it is needed to account for all movement and relative changes. It is both transcendent and immanent, and monism (theism) and pantheism are not clearly separated.

Aristotle was later to observe that Anaxagoras invoked Mind (*Nous*) only when mechanical explanations failed. It would appear that mechanical explanations were available, but for some reason he rejected them. Anaxagoras was a creative and radical thinker. As the one who introduced Mind as an explanatory principle, he laid the foundation for philosophical idealism which was to reach a high level of expression in Plato. He raised the issue of "the best possible of worlds," to be explored by Leibnitz. Finally, he raised serious questions about the cyclical view of history, thus laying the groundwork for a progressive view of history.

The Cosmologists

Before moving to the Sophists, who mark the transition from nature to humanity, we look briefly at a group of cosmologists. These thinkers advocated an "atomic theory" of the universe. Their insights remain influential in natural-scientific views of the universe today. They present quantative views of reality.

Leucippus and Democritus were co-founders of this school of cosmology. Their theories are so inseparable that it is not easy to sort out their individual contributions.

Aristotle tells us that Leucippus was the founder of this school. Tradition has it that Leucippus came from Miletus, studied under Zeno of Elea and established this school at Abdura where Democritus became his most famous disciple. If Leucippus did originate the theory, it is generally believed that Democritus made the school famous, being the most famous disciple of Leucippus. Thus we turn to Democritus as the key representative of the cosmologists.

Democritus was born in 460 B.C. and died in 370 B.C. He travelled extensively and wrote books on physics, metaphysics, ethics, history and mathematics.

The cosmologists, also known as the atomists, agree with the Eleatics that absolute change does not occur. But they observe that things are in constant motion. They reason that motion and change are not possible without empty space or what Parmenides called non-being. Hence, they insist that non-being (empty space) is a fact of existence. Empty space, however, is not identical with corporeal (material) things. Yet it does possess a kind of reality. Bodies are no more real than space, for a thing can be real without being a body.

Atoms and the empty space in which they move are the sole realities for these thinkers: everything is either plenum or void. Being, or the full, and non-being, or the void, are equally real. The real is not one continuous, undivided, immoveable being, as the Eleatics held. It is a plurality, an infinite number of beings, separated from one another by empty space.

Each of these beings is indivisible, impenetrable, and simple. The atom is not a mathematical point of a center of force. Atoms are alike in quality—however, they are not earth, air, fire and water. They are very small physical units, differing in shape, size, weight, arrangements and position. Atoms are underived, indestructible and unchangeable.

Atoms remind us of the indivisible being of Parmenides broken into small bits that cannot be further divided. Each atom possesses the eternity, unchangeability and indivisibility which Parmenides ascribed to his single being.

According to Democritus, these atoms which are separated from each other by empty spaces are the building stones of reality from which the different objects are formed—they are combined and recombined in different ways. All bodies are combinations of atoms and spaces: origin means union; destruction, separation.

Atoms act on one another by direct contact only, through pressure and impact, or by means of emanations moving from one body and striking another. Any action at a distance is excluded by this atomic hypothesis. What causes atoms to unite and separate is the motion inherent in them. The motion of the atoms is governed by inexorable mechanical laws.

The inherent motion of the atoms is uncaused, like the atoms themselves—they have never been at rest, but have been in motion from the beginning. Space cannot be the cause of motion; hence motion must be regarded as an inherent property of each atom. Atoms are different shapes and sizes, and they interlace and hook together. It is in this manner that physical objects made up of larger grouping of atoms are formed. Atoms have no other qualities except impenetrability, shape and size.

Atoms are known through thought rather than sense perception. Sense perception does not yield true knowledge of things—it indicates only how things affect us. The atomists anticipate the distinction between primary qualities (impenetrability, shape) and secondary qualities (i.e., color, sound, smell). But they insisted that we cannot *see* atoms. We must *think* them. Hence they insist that sense-perception is an obscure form of knowledge. Thought, however, transcends our senses and appearances and reaches the atoms. Thought for the atomists is genuine knowledge.

Democritus does not discount the importance of sense-perception. Reason begins where sense-perception ends. Reason is said to be the highest function of the soul. The soul and reason are the same.

According to Democritus, gods also exist. Gods, like humans, are composed of atoms. But they have a long life, are more powerful, and possess reason on a higher order than humans. Gods are also subject to the impersonal law of the motion of atoms.

Democritus, like many of his contemporaries, was a rationalist. His insistence upon the superiority of reason over sense extended into ethics. The end of all conduct is well-being. Well-being is defined not as pleasure but as the satisfaction which accompanies the exercise of the rational faculties.

He should do right from a sense of duty rather than from a fear of punishment. A good person does not merely refrain from doing wrong, but also loses the desire to do wrong. The best way to achieve the good life is to exercise our mental powers, through reflection and the contemplation of beautiful acts.

It is surprising that a materialistic and naturalistic philosophy represented by the cosmologists should end up in this manner. What we have found among the atomists are exalted insights on psychology, epistemology, theology and ethics. Many important aspects of classical theology and philosophy are here in a seminal form.

Summary: The Cosmological Stage of Greek Philosophy (Pre-Socratic)

The preoccupation with external nature extends between 600 and 450 B.C. and beyond. The scene of this period is the Greek colonial world, which included Greece itself together with Ionia, Southern Italy and Sicily.

This philosophy is mainly *naturalistic*: its attention is directed to nature. It is *hylozoistic*: it conceives of nature as animated or alive. It is *ontological*: it inquires into the essence of things. It is *epistemological*: it is concerned with the source and nature of the knowledge of things. It is *monistic*: it seeks to explain phenomena by means of a single principle. And, it is *dogmatic*: it presupposes the competence of the human mind to solve the problem of the world.

The philosophers of the naturalistic period were concerned with two interdependent or interrelated problems regarding external nature. The first problem is relates to *substance*. What is the basic substance or substances of which natural objects are constituted and from which they originate? The second was the problem of change. What is the nature of the process by which the basic substance(s) change into the objects of sense? The reflections of these philosophers upon the ultimate grounds of existence as well as the relation of all things prepared the way for the history of human thought henceforth, at least in the West.

III

Classical Greek Philosophy[1]

The Sophists

In a technical sense, we do not reach the classical period of Greek philosophy until we examine the thought of Socrates, Plato and Aristotle. But the transition in philosophical thinking which the Sophists represent is the basis for the later development. We need, therefore, look briefly at their contribution. The Sophists pushed thought beyond the naturalistic philosophers. They represent the spirit of free inquiry which took them into many fields of thought. The following three examples are representative of their broad intellectual interests.

There were dramatic poets like Aeschylus (525–453 B.C.), Sophocles (496–405 B.C.,) and Euripides (480–406 B.C.) who reflected this new influence. Their views on life and religion were deepened and broadened by criticism and reflection. Historians and geographers like Herodotus (born 480 B.C.) and Thucydides (born 471 B.C.) moved beyond legendary tales and superstitions. These authors gave classical expression to ancient folklore. And, finally, in medicine many ideas and practices were abandoned. There was a desire for better knowledge of the human body. Many philosophers were also physicians. They applied their physical theories to the art of healing. Hippocrates (born 460 B.C.) is still known for the impact he made upon the scientific study of medicine.

This was an important period because of its criticism of the past and its preparation for the future. There was a temporary lull in building systems of thought. In the meantime, everything was being questioned—i.e. the origin and purpose of the state, moral conduct, art and education. The spirit of independence and critical thought invaded most fields and prepared the way for the greater era of speculative thought to come.

The period has appropriately been called the Enlightenment. The Persian Wars (500–449 B.C.) left Athens as the mistress of the seas and a world power. She was the commercial, intellectual and artistic center of Greece. Poets, artists, teachers and philosophers entered her gates and helped to entertain and instruct her wealthy citizens. A list of illustrious persons comes to mind: Pericles, Anaxagoras, Thucydides, Phidias, Sophocles, Euripides, Aristophanes, Hippocrates and Socrates. Thus Pericles in a great funeral oration declared Athens to be the "School of Greece."

Along with this new cultural revival and intellectual freedom came a desire for power and its results—i.e. wealth, fame, culture, efficiency and success. Relativism set in as foundations were questioned and traditional views on religion, morality, politics, philosophy and science were abandoned. People wanted to be informed on new subjects. Public life offered novel opportunities for persons who could persuade and convince others of their ideas. As a result, there was a great demand for rhetoric, oratory and dialectic.

Individualism thrived, but it was an individualism set loose from the authority of the group. Each person was free to think and act, to win personal salvation as independent of old traditions. This state of affairs inevitably led to disputes and tended toward intellectual subjectivism and ethical relativism. For example: "What I think is true, *is* true; what I believe is right, *is* right." Thus skepticism ruled the theoretical sphere, while self-interest was preached in the practical field.

This new movement was represented by the Sophists. The term *sophist* originally meant a wise and skillful person, but in time it took on a different meaning. It was applied to the professional teachers who travelled about giving instructions for pay in the art of thinking, speaking and the preparation of young men for public life. It often became a title used for ridicule because of the radical teachings of some Sophists.

Some Sophists boasted that they could change the minds of their pupils in a very short time. They were well schooled in grammar, rhetoric, oratory and dialectics. They broke new ground for theoretical as well as practical thought. In addition, the Sophists raised important issues which led to more systematic and thorough treatment—i.e. a theory of the state. But on the whole many of these teachers were satisfied merely to teach their pupils how to subdue an opponent by any means available—even to make the worse appear better and to confound others with logical fallacies.

The Sophists did not accept the conclusions of the nature philosophers who preceded them. With these later thinkers, philosophy became self-critical. They were aware of the limitations of the human faculty of thought and raised the question whether it is capable of grappling with the problems propounded by the cosmologists. The Sophists turned to the human subject. For them, knowledge depends upon the knower—a particular person. What is true to that person, *is* true for that person. There is no objective truth, but only subjective opinion.

Protagoras, one of the greatest of the Sophists, declared: "man is the measure of all things." This relativistic doctrine of the human person as the measure of all things repudiates the paradoxical conclusions of Parmenides and Zeno—in favor of the judgments of the individual person. The individual is autonomous in matters of knowledge. Two statements which contradict each other may be true, though one could be *better* that the other. In making the latter judgment, Protagoras seems to want to recall standards he has denied.

Gorgias, another noted Sophist, took the extreme position, viz., that none of these individual statements are true. In his work titled *On Nature* or the *Nonexistent*, he reasons thus: 1. there is nothing; 2. even if there is something we could not know it; and 3. even if it existed and we could know it, we could not communicate this knowledge to others. This is close to nihilism. This is the logical drift of sophistry.

And, yet, all is not negative. Their clever and ingenious thinking does pave the way for classical Greek thought. They recognized the practical aspect of knowledge. While they denounced absolute theoretical thought, they insisted that the relative knowledge of individuals has a practical influence upon the conduct of the ordinary affairs of life.

The Sophists move logically from intellectual skepticism to ethical skepticism. If knowledge is impossible, then the knowledge of right and wrong is also unavailable. The diversity of customs, morals and traditions of various nations led the Sophists to question the validity of absolute objective standards of conduct and social action.

Protagoras (born c. 490 B.C.) hesitated at this ethical relativism. He insisted that all established institutions, including law and morality, were merely conventional, but necessary. He held that certain legal and moral rules *must* be adhered to, if there is to be any moral order at all. Gorgias appeared at times also to make reservations to his extreme statements on morals. Both Protagoras and Gorgias make the important distinction between "nature" and "convention." In this regard, they paved the way for subsequent development of Greek thought.

Some radical views were inevitable. The floodgate of ideas had been opened and the drift toward ethical nihilism was the result. The concept that "might is right" and the "survival of the fittest" surfaced amongst the Sophists. Laws were now viewed as not being grounded in the nature of things; they were arbitrary agreements among humans. Some concluded that it is to the advantage of the strong individual to impose laws on others so that they make break them.

It may come as a surprise to find so many seminal ideas amongst the Sophists. For example, they anticipate the pragmatism so well-known in William James and John Dewey—indeed in the American outlook. Beyond this, in the nihilism and other aspects of the thought of the Sophists we see ideas which surface in thinkers like Machiavelli, Nietzsche, Darwin, Spencer, Malthus, William Shockley, and even Hitler.

It would appear that the contribution to philosophy by the Sophists was more in method than in substance. They produced a climate which gave direction to the great philosophers to come. They awakened and challenged philosophy, religion, customs, morals and institutions to justify themselves to reason. They forced philosophy to examine the thinking process itself. Philosophy was driven to first principles. What is right? What is good? What is the meaning and purpose of the state and of human institutions? What is the nature of the world and the human place in nature? These problems are the essence of philosophy. They place us squarely upon the doorsteps of Socrates, Plato and Aristotle.

Socrates

Socrates: The Man

Socrates was born in Athens in 469 B.C. His parents were poor. His father was a sculptor and his mother was a midwife. We do not know how he acquired his education, but it is obvious that he grew intellectually in Athens. At first he took up his father's occupation, but soon felt a divine call to examine himself and question others regarding ultimate questions. He conversed with all sorts of people, on the streets, in the marketplace, in gymnasia. His subjects were diverse: war, politics, marriage, friendship, love, the fine arts, trades, poetry, religion, science, etc. He was preoccupied with life and life-situations. His interest was limited so far as physical things like trees and stones were concerned. Human life was his domain.

Socrates possessed a subtle, keen and sharp intellect and he could easily penetrate the minds of others. He would discover the fallacies in their arguments and direct the conversation to the heart of the matter. He was said to have been kind and gentle and with good humor. He was however, decisive in exposing superficiality with wit and logic.

During a long life of seventy years, Socrates revealed moral courage, in war as well as in the pursuit of his political duties. He lived an exemplary life according to the virtues he taught. He manifested self-control, nobility, frugality, patience and simplicity in his own life.

His trial and death are an index to his character. Socrates displayed moral dignity as well as firmness and conviction as he faced a tragic end. He did what he thought was right, without fear or favor. He died as impressively as he had lived, with love for all and malice toward none. Condemned by his own people, Socrates was forced to drink a poisonous cup of hemlock (399 B.C.). He was accused falsely of atheism and the corruption of youth in Athens. He could have escaped, as his friends had arranged this. But Socrates respected the authority of the state and would not prove disloyal to such laws to save his own life. He firmly believed that he should live and even die according to what he taught others.

Socrates was not attractive in personal appearance. He was short, stocky, stout, bleary-eyed and snub-nosed. He had a large mouth and was careless in dress and also clumsy. He was not handsome, especially by Greek standards. But when he spoke, so great was his wisdom and personal charm that everyone he encountered seemed to be drawn to him by his unusual intellect and the effectiveness of his words.

Socrates wrote nothing, yet he was an outstanding thinker, who through his greatest disciple Plato has exerted an invaluable influence upon all Western philosophy. We are faced with an insoluble problem when we attempt to distinguish the real historical

Socrates from the Socrates we meet in the dialogues of Plato. We should neither consider Socrates' contribution as a mere stage in Plato's system nor attribute to Socrates all that Plato says he taught. An in-between view is best. Socrates appears to have invented the philosophical method of conceptual analysis and definition expressed in Plato's dialogues. But he seems to have been mainly interested in the application of this method to ethical thought and behavior.

The Socratic Problem

Socrates met the challenge of the Sophists. The Sophists, as Socrates viewed the situation, threatened the very foundations of morality and the state. He wanted to counter the skepticism of the age, and escape the nihilistic implications of his time. He considered the prevailing ethical and political fallacies as based upon a misconception of truth. There was a need to define the problem of knowledge in order to overcome this confused situation. This conviction together with his faith in human reason formed his sense of vocation. His task was not to build a philosophical system. He desired to arouse in others the love of truth and virtue. He saw a correspondence between correct thinking and right living. He sought the correct method to acquire knowledge for practical application. He lived what he thought, and taught others to follow the truth.

In order to engage the problem before him, Socrates brought life, thought and conduct together. The Sophists said there is no truth, and that knowledge is unattainable. Humans differ from one another. One opinion is set against another and one opinion is just as good as another. This assumption was vigorously opposed by Socrates. He agreed that there is diversity of thought, but he insisted that we must seek agreement at the bedrock. There is a need for some principle as a common ground for truth and goodness.

According to Socrates, if we would reach truth, we must not trust every chance opinion that enters our heads. Confused, vague, empty, thoughts fill our minds. We have a lot of undigested opinions which we have accepted on faith, of which we do not understand the meaning. There are a lot of arbitrary assertions for which we have no warrant. According to Socrates, our most ardent task is to make ideas clear, to understand the real meaning of terms, to define correctly the notions we employ and to know exactly what we are talking about. Then we should have reasons for our views, prove our assertions and be able to think rather than guess. We could then put our theories to the test of verification by the facts and modify and correct them as well.

The Socratic Method

The purpose of the Socratic method was to evolve universal judgments. In his discussions, Socrates used an ingenious form of cross-examination. He pretended not to know any more about the subject than others in the conversation. He often even professed not to know anything or less than those who put questions to him (Socratic irony). Yet these latter were soon to feel that Socrates was the master of the situation. His discussants were caught in self-contradictions as he guided them toward a different understanding of life and truth. He was the master teacher. The confused saw their ideas take shape, become clear, and stand out like beautiful statues. Just as his father was a sculptor in stone, Socrates was a sculptor of thought and life. And again, just as his mother was a midwife, Socrates gave birth to ideas.

Socrates began his discussion with popular ideas and opinions. He would test these by illustrations from everyday life, showing where possible that these were not well-founded. He would point out the need for modification and correction. He would then assist those in the conversation to correct themselves. By means of relevant examples, he would lead them step by step to new insights and truth. His method made use of skillful questioning.

For example, Socrates gets a young man named Euthydemus to confess his ambition to become a great politician and stateman. Socrates then suggests to him that in order to pursue his ambition, he must hope to become a just man. The young man thinks that he is already just (Xenophon, *Mem.*, IV, ch. 2). But at the end of the conversation with Socrates, he is no longer sure of his justness. Euthydemus has lost confidence in his answers. Everything now seems opposite to what he had previously imagined. Socrates was thus able to teach him and guide him to a different self-understanding as well as to a more exalted understanding of what it meant to be just.

According to Socrates, knowledge is possible if one employs a correct method. Socrates, however, did not carefully define his method. His method takes its form as he used it. We are left, therefore, with a description. We observe that Socrates would carefully define terms correctly and carry reasoning back to first principles. Like the Sophists, Socrates was not interested in metaphysical speculation or cosmological concerns. He never wearied, however, in his search for answer to moral questions: What is piety? What is beauty? What is just or unjust? What is courage or cowardice? What is a statesman or a good citizen? These were his type of questions. They were human topics. It was his view that if we did not engage these questions we would become slaves.

Socratic Ethics

Socrates sought a rational basis for conduct. He stood between contemporary radicals and conservatives. The former group considered ethical ideas and practices as mere conventions. They concluded that might makes right. Conservatives, on the other hand, saw morality as self-evident. Reason has nothing to say about these matters. They must be obeyed.

These views did not satisfy Socrates. He wanted to understand the meaning of morality. He sought a rational principle of right and wrong. In his view, there must be a criterion by which to decide moral issues. He inquired: How can we order life? What is the rational way to live? How ought a rational (a reasoning) being to act? The Sophists were not right in their assertion that human beings are the measure of all things. They asserted that what pleases me, the particular person, is right and there is no universal good. Over against this, Socrates argues that there must be some principle or standard, or good, which all rational creatures recognize and accept. There is *the* good, which is the good for the sake of which all else is good, the highest good.

According to Socrates, knowledge is the highest good. Knowledge is virtue. Right thinking is essential to right action. Unless one knows what virtue is, the meaning of self-control, courage, justice, piety and their opposites, one cannot be virtuous. But, knowing what virtue is, one will be virtuous. Knowledge is the necessary and sufficient condition for virtue. Socrates assumed that no one is voluntarily bad or good. To prefer evil is not native to humans. He did not believe that we will deliberately choose the greater of two evils. He was not convinced that in the face of knowledge, humans will choose evil. If we know what is good, we will choose it. For Socrates, right and wrong were not mere theoretical opinions. Moral choices were a matter of practical conviction. They were not matters of intellect alone, they were supported by the will.

The virtuous life is the best way to live. Holding that virtue is knowledge led Socrates to assert the oneness or unity of knowledge.

The several virtues are but different forms of virtue as such. Virtue is not only good in itself—it is in our best interest. The tendency of all honorable and useful actions is to make life painless and pleasant. The honorable is useful and good. Virtue and true happiness are identical. In order to be happy one must embrace temperance, courage, wisdom and justice.

The Socratic Influence

Socrates still lives through his contribution to philosophical method and ethics. There was an immediate impact of Socrates in the sphere of ethics. He lives on in the work of Plato and to a lesser degree through Aristotle. We need not treat his contribution through Plato or Aristotle here. This will become obvious as we move forward in this study. Here I shall briefly show how his influence flows through the early ethical tradition.

The Cyrenaic and Cynic schools emphasized different aspects of the thought of Socrates. The Cyrenaic school was founded by Aristippus (born ca. 435) at Cyrene. The Cynic school was established by Antishthenes (died 366) at the gymnasium of Cynosarges in Athens.

The Cyrenaics seized upon Socrates' emphasis on the joy and satisfaction of the intellectual life. The highest good, *summum bonum*, became for them the attainment of the greatest amount of pleasure as well as the avoidance of pain. Therefore, the Cyrenaics were known for the doctrine of pure hedonism. They did not make a qualitative distinction between higher or lower pleasures. They advocated the pursuit of those pleasures which are more intense, whether of the body, mind or soul. Unfortunately, this type of hedonism has in itself the germ of pessimism. To pursue pleasure as an end in itself is frustrated by the real life which includes some pain. Furthermore, the exclusive pursuit of pleasure leads to boredom, meaninglessness and sometimes nihilism. It is instructive that Hegesius, a member of this school, concluded that suicide is the only way out of life's tragic situation. He observed that most people experience more pain/than pleasure—thus he encouraged people to commit suicide. What is most important is to be aware of the misunderstanding of the fundamentals of Socrates' ethical thought.

The Cynics took Socrates' thesis on virtue as their point of departure. They agreed that virtue is knowledge. They went on to assert that virtue is its own reward. Virtue is good in itself apart from any consideration of pleasure or pain. They took the view that virtue is knowledge to the extreme. Virtue is to be independent of all want and void of pleasure. This led to unusual discipline, restraint, renunciation, poverty and asceticism. Some rejected civilized life and sought a return to nature. This rigid form of life was embraced by Diogenes of Sinope. Again, the view is one-sided and does not fully capture the original meaning of the ethics of Socrates.

Finally, what these two schools held in common was admiration for Socrates as well as a desire to save the individual. The Cyrenaics sought to do this through the pursuit of pleasure, while the Cynics attempted to accomplish the same goal through the renunciation of pleasure or through self-control. The two schools influenced the development of ethics in the post-classical period of Greek philosophy, that is, after Aristotle. The Cyrenaics made an impression upon the Epicureans who adopted and modified the pleasure principle. The Stoics were influenced by the Cynics in a similar manner.

Plato

The problems suggested by Socrates had to be thought out to the end. They were intimately connected with one another and with the problem of the ultimate nature of being. No adequate answer was possible unless these problems were studied in their inter-relations and as parts of a larger question. The problems of the meaning of human life, knowledge, conduct and institutions were Socrates' interests. Plato embraced the problems, but insisted that complete answers to the above set of problems depends upon the meaning reality as a whole. Plato sought a theory of the entire universe.

Plato's lifetime, 427–347 B.C., was marked by many changes in social and political affairs. The Peloponnesian War, the eventual victory of Athens over Sparta with the aid of the Persians, the expansion of Athenian power and the rise of Philip of Macedonia, were notable events of Plato's life.

Plato came from an aristocratic family. On his father's side he inherited a royal background, since his father was a descendant of the kings of Athens. On his mother's side, there was also an exalted lineage. Plato had several relatives who were politically active as aristocrats. He was exposed to the best educational opportunities, was an excellent athlete and military man. He was interested in Homer and the fine arts. Plato's conversion to philosophy was gradual and over a sustained period of time. When he came under the influence his life was changed. It was the death of Socrates which finally transformed his life.

Many details of Plato's life do not stand on solid historical evidence. But some events seem to be reflected in his writings. It is, for example, reported that he travelled widely in Egypt, Asia Minor and Italy. He is said to have encountered the Pythagoreans and that his first teacher of philosophy was Cratylus, a Heraclitean thinker.

It is assumed that Plato did establish a school known as the Academy. There he taught mathematics and philosophy through lectures and dialogues. He was a poet and mystic as well as a philosopher and dialectician. Plato possessed great powers of logical analysis and abstract thought—these often blended with the poetic imagination and deep mystical feeling.

Tradition has it that Plato lived for a time at the court of Dionysus I, the tyrant of Syracuse. He is reported to have been rejected by this ruler and to have become a prisoner of war. Then, during the years 367–361 B.C., he is said to have returned twice to Syracuse with the hope that an ideal state might be established. He was disappointed in that expectation and died in 347 B.C. In sum, Plato was noble of character, an aristocrat by birth, an idealist and a person of exemplary character.

Within the framework of Plato's system, we have a combination and transformation of the Greek thinkers until his time. We recall many influences from prior philosophical developments. We note that he agrees that the Sophists were correct in asserting that knowledge restricted to appearance is impossible. With Socrates he argues that genuine knowledge is by concepts. Heraclitus was right to point out that the world is in constant change. On the other hand, the Eleatics were correct as they held that ideas are unchangeable. The atomists were on target as they saw being as manifold. Plato agreed with most of his Greek predecessors that knowledge is rational. With Anaxagoras, Plato reasoned that mind is distinct from matter and that mind (*nous*) is the controlling principle. Through these instances we see in Plato the convergence of cardinal ideas in Greek philosophy before his time. But Plato's thought is more than a syncretistic summary of Greek ideas, it is a creative and constructive system reaching forth into an unknown future.

It is not possible to arrange Plato's writings in chronological order. But it is possible to distinguish his earlier writing (with much dependence on Socrates) from his own later contribution. In works

like the *Apology*, *Crito* and *Protagoras*, Plato seems to rely heavily
upon the views of Socrates. In *Phaedrus*, *Meno*, *Georgias*, *Sophistes*
and *Parmenides*, he begins to develop his own views and to work
out his own method. Finally, in the *Symposium*, *Phaedo*, *Republic*,
Timaeus and *Laws*, Plato completes his system. Plato's writings
come to us in dialogues, while his lectures have disappeared.

Plato's Theory of Knowledge

According to Plato, knowledge begins with *opinion*. This arises
out of *imagination*. At the outset knowledge is imperfect — it is hazy,
indefinite and vague. The separation of fact from illusion is difficult.
There is little difference between internal and external sensation,
and the distinction between subjective and objective viewpoints is
not clear.

After opinion comes *assurance* or *confidence*. In the second stage,
we learn to describe *objective phenomena*. Thought now becomes
more distinct and is more clearly defined. We sense a difference
between our views and the external world, on this level of knowledge. We observe phenomena outside ourselves which are not
controlled by our wishes. But, knowledge is not yet unified —
we merely perceive an unending flux. We share the universe as
Heraclitus perceived it. The third stage of knowledge is *intelligent
understanding*. We enter the province of real knowledge now. We
are able to describe phenomena — a relationship is established
between cause and effect. We are able to use our scientific resources
at this stage. We overcome chaos and disorder and we now observe
that there are natural laws which the universe obeys. This provides
us with a measure of control over the forces of nature.

Sense experience, however, does not give us a concept of true
reality because of its limitations. Being dependent upon sense
knowledge, its acceptance of first principles does not provide a
complete view of nature. It is preoccupied with concrete objects and
phenomena. According to Plato, knowledge at its highest must
transcend natural phenomena as well as concrete representations.

The fourth stage is reason that is freed from the bondage of sense.
This is the level of *dialectic* or *philosophy*. Philosophy leaves the
realm of phenomena behind — it is concerned with immaterial *Form*.
Reason gives order and unity. It brings together all the other aspects
of knowledge. It produces a view of the interrelationship and
interdependence of knowledge.

The fifth stage of knowledge transcends reason — it involves the mind in *mystical intuition*, by which one obtains a vision of the unintelligible realm of Ideas. This involves the transformation of our inner being. At the same time, it negates the limitations of time and space. We now become part of the absolute realm of beauty and truth. Thus a strain of mysticism enters Plato's epistemological schema.

An example of the progression of knowledge in Plato as described above is illustrated in his allegory of the cave in the *Republic*, Book Seven. The task of knowledge is liberation from the underground cave of the sensible world, which contains merely a collection of physical objects. We cannot be satisfied until we reach the realm of Forms in the world above, which contain all knowledge. In the cave we see only our own reflections—vague shadows which create an atmosphere of unreality. Above, in the intelligible realm we are enlightened by the Ideas, and obtain a true knowledge.

Recollection or Reminiscence

The apprehension of ideas known in a previous existence can be traced directly to Socrates. Plato's doctrine of recollection related to this has just been discussed. When we raise the questions, How do we understand universal Ideas? Where does this knowledge come from? and How is it possible? Plato would respond that it is not in the phenomenal world, where we must depend upon sense objects. These are transitory, as Heraclitus had said. Plato offers as his explanation the doctrine of recollection, especially as it is discussed in *Meno*. We are reminded of the universal objects which we saw before we were born. Our souls, before entering the physical body, had a view of eternal forms. We are vaguely aware of those forms in our present existence. Certain universal principles are innate or *a priori*. These are not derived from our physical environment.

Throughout the history of Western philosophy there have been, after Plato, those who accept his view on *a priori* knowledge. But there have also been those like Locke who believe that the mind is a *tabla rasa* or blank tablet upon which experience writes. In general, Plato's outlook is rationalistic—it exalts universal principles. His view led to mysticism. This is especially true of neo-Platonism, which in turn influenced Augustine.

ontology – science of BEING
teleology – doctrine of final causes or purposes

Plato's Doctrine of Ideas

According to Plato, this material world, known through sensation, is the realm of becoming and change. It is not the object of knowledge. We can have no certain understanding of it. We can only form opinions which are bound to be fallacious. Reality is *immaterial* and is described by infallible laws. We are to be reminded, however, that reality must satisfy our aesthetic needs. It is not mechanistic; for it must fulfill our desire for absolute perfection. The Sophists stressed the existence of particular things, which individuals could judge as true or false. Gorgias, for instance, had gone so far as to assert that there is no reality. Plato, to the contrary, insisted that reality does exist. It is the true source of all being and all knowledge.

Plato exalts the universal over the particular. This view is at the center of his system of thought. Knowledge is not preoccupied with individual things—it is concerned about essences (Universal Forms). The particular aspect of things does not last. It is merged into the flux; but Forms (Ideas) have an eternal existence.

Ideas, according to Plato, have no corporeal status. They are uncreated—they do not come into existence, nor do they pass away. They always exist. They are perfect, absolute and are not subject to the limitations of the senses.

Ideas are also *ideals.* They are objects of aspiration. The idea of beauty is a standard for all evaluation. Ideas are not only *ontological,* they are teleological as well. Ideas are not limited, however, to mental and intellectual values; they refer to physical objects as well—i.e. chairs and houses.

Reason rather than opinion leads to knowledge of Ideas. Ideas are archetypes; they make up a well-ordered world or a rational cosmos. They are arranged in logical order and are subsumed under the Idea of the Good. The Idea of the Good is supreme among Ideas and is the ultimate source of all. The truly real and truly good are the same. The Idea of the Good is the *logos* or cosmic purpose. Again, in the world of Ideas, unity includes plurality. There is no unity without plurality and no plurality without unity. The universe is a logical system of Ideas, governed by a universal purpose, the Idea of the Good.

Plato's theory of Ideas is an original philosophical achievement. The Pythagorean number-mysticism, the eternal being of Parmenides, the Heraclitean *logos*-doctrine, the *nous* of Anaxagoras and the concepts of Socrates are all found in Plato's ideal theory. But the theory as a well stated metaphysical position is due to the genius of Plato.

Plato on Matter

In contrast to Ideas, matter is perishable, imperfect and unreal. It is non-being. Any reality, form, beauty that the perceived world may have is derived from Ideas. The sensible world partakes of a measure of reality or being, insofar as it takes on form. Things owe their being to the presence in them of Ideas. That is to say, they can *participate* in Ideas. At the same time, non-being, the substratum, is responsible for the imperfection of many different objects embodying the same Ideas.

Matter is a dull, irrational and recalcitrant force. Plato refers to it as an unwilling slave which takes on (imperfectly) the impress of the idea. Matter in relation to the Idea is both friend and foe. It is both an auxiliary and an obstruction to Ideas. Plato attributes physical as well as moral evil to matter. It also accounts for imperfection and change.

Plato has thus set up a dualism between Idea and matter. The world of Ideas is the source of goodness. It is the paramount principle of things. But, on the contrary, matter is responsible for non-being, imperfection and evil. Matter is an inferior and secondary principle. Ideas point to reality, while matter indicates appearance. Neither is reducible to the other.

Plato's Cosmology

Plato continues the cosmological speculations of the pre-Socratics, but includes some mythical elements as well. Plato projects a comprehensive system of thought of all time and all existence. His cosmology is part of his intention.

According to Plato, the Demiurge fashions a world according to the pattern of the ideal world, guided by the Idea of the Good. He forms as perfect a universe as possible, being hampered by matter. The Demiurge, described by Plato in his *Timaeus*, is an architect rather than a creator. This is so, because both the ideal and the material are available to be used—they do not wait to be created. The function of the Demiurge is to impose form on matter which already exists.

In addition, Plato asserts that the world is composed of four material elements (earth, air, fire, water) and an animate soul—a world-soul. The world-soul is composed of identity and change and is able to know the ideal as well as perceive the material. It is an intermediary between the world of Ideas and the world of phenomena. Plato assumed that the gods were created and he refers to many gods. The Demiurge created the rational soul, leaving it for the lesser gods to create the irrational soul of man and the lower creatures. He does not ascribe personality to any divine being. His cosmology includes many gods, the world of Ideas (i.e. the Idea of the Good), the Demiurge, the world-soul, the planetary souls, the gods of popular religion, etc.

Plato's cosmology is a teleological world-view clothed in mythical garb. He attempted to explain reality as a purposeful, well-ordered cosmos. The world is intelligent and is guided by reason toward an ethical goal. Purposes are final causes—they are the real causes of the world. Physical causes merely cooperate with them. The rational, the good, the purposeful are explained through reason. Whatever is evil, irrational, purposeless is traceable to matter.

The influence of Plato is great whether we look to Aristotle, Neo-Platonism or Christian theology (Augustine or Aquinas). His cosmology has exerted a continuous influence in the West.

Plato's Psychology

We now look at Plato's understanding of the body/soul dualism. In sensation and opinion, the soul is dependent on the body. But the soul in its own right belongs to the world of Ideas or pure reason. The body, in fact, is an impediment to knowledge, from which the soul must be set free in order to lay hold upon truth in its purity.

The soul possesses knowledge from its pre-existence. All knowledge is *anamnesis* or reminiscence—reawakening. The soul existed prior to inhabiting the body. The human soul is in part pure reason. The rational part is the most characteristic aspect of the soul. The union with the body is a hindrance to the intellectual aspirations of the soul. The ascendancy of reason in the soul is hampered by the presence of impulses and desires in the body.

Plato separates the soul into rational and irrational parts. He then breaks the irrational into *spirited* and *appetitive* divisions. The former is *dualistic*, while the latter is tripartite. The rational faculty is intellectual and accounts for such things as gentleness, humility and the like. The spirited faculty is the directing faculty. It is a dynamic entity and in this regard resembles the will. It is characterized by such matters as ambition and anger. The appetitive faculty points to desire. It is represented by such things as bodily appetites. Desires for pleasure, wealth or food are examples of the expressions of the appetitive faculty. But pleasure for Plato can be on a higher quality level. It can be manifest in beauty and goodness as well as through physical activities. The soul functions through its faculties, which are distinct principles. There can, however, be interplay or cooperation between faculties. Here are a few examples: Reason may restrain thirst when water is impure. The spirited faculty rebels against morbid bodily appetites. In the case of a moderate desire for food or drink, the spirited faculty may be an ally of reason. Plato goes on to insist the soul possess a unity despite the plurality of its faculties.

On the Immortality of the Soul

According to Plato the soul is immortal. This is so because of the soul's knowledge of the forms. Only like can know like. The forms or Ideas are eternal and, therefore, the soul must also be. The soul, being pre-existent, is also post-existent. In *Meno*, Socrates questions a slave boy who provides proof of a geometrical theorum which he had not been taught. Socrates assumes that the soul had this knowledge before birth. Plato develops these insights of his mentor Socrates with reference to the soul's immortality.

There are several reasons why Plato asserts that the soul is immortal. The soul is the principle of life. Life cannot come from death. The soul is the source of motion. It is self-moving. This motion is perpetual or eternal. The world as a moral, rational and just order demands a future life of rewards and punishments for the rectification of imperfections in life.

Under the influence of Orphic and Pythagorean mysticism, Plato develops a doctrine of transmigration of souls (metempsychosis). The soul (rational) once inhabited a star. It became obsessed with a desire for the world of sense and became imprisoned in a material body. The soul will either return to its lofty abode or sink lower into successive bodies of different animals. Had the soul resisted sense desire it would have retained its exalted status where it contemplated ideas.

Finally, we observe that Plato's psychology treats the doctrine of eros. The perception of sensuous beauty, which excites sense love, revives the soul's memory of ideal beauty in its former existence. These recollections of truth and beauty inspire a yearning for the higher life of the world of pure ideas. So this same eros in its higher manifestation creates science, art and noble human institutions.

I have presented a sketch of the important ideas of Plato with the understanding that all philosophy in the West remains in his debt. As our discussion develops, we will recall when appropriate his ideas as they influence the reflection of philosophers and theologians in our project. I turn now to Aristotle, Plato's most famous disciple. But we will also observe that Aristotle is a creative and original thinker in his own right.

Aristotle

Plato's philosophy was comprehensive, but it left difficulties to be resolved and inconsistencies to be overcome. Since Plato's thought was passed on mainly as it had been received, Aristotle assumes the task of a more systematic presentation. Aristotle was Plato's greatest pupil, with an independent mind. He set out to reconstruct the system of Plato and to restate it in a more consistent and scientific manner.

Aristotle was born (384 B.C.) in Stagira. He was the son of Nicomachus, the court physician of Macedon. He entered Plato's Academy at seventeen. He remained there as student and teacher for twenty years. After Plato died, Aristotle travelled extensively, and subsequently returned to Athens, where he opened a school of rhetoric. In 342 he was enlisted by King Philip of Macedon to direct the education of his son Alexander, later known as the Great. Seven years later, Aristotle returned to Athens, where he established a school dedicated to Lycean Apollo. The school was known as the Lyceum. It is also referred to as the Peripatetic school because of Aristotle's habit of walking while giving instruction. He taught by means of both lecture and dialogue. After the sudden death of Alexander in 323, Aristotle was accused of sacrilege by the anti-Macedonian party at Athens and forced to flee to Euboea, where he died in 322 B.C.

Aristotle is said to have been a man of noble character. He realized in his own life and personality the Greek ideal of balance and harmony taught in his ethics. He loved truth and was strong and sober in his judgment. He as a masterful dialectician, a lover of detail and a close observer of facts. His literary style was sober and free of fantasy. There is a lack of sparkle in his personality and writings. He was not given to expressive emotion. In this regard he differs from Plato. His writings portray a person who was calm and impersonal in his reasoning. Aristotle is, nevertheless, one of the most outstanding thinkers of all time—a universal genius. He wrote learnedly on many subjects: logic, rhetoric, poetics, botany, zoology, psychology, ethics, economics, politics and metaphysics.

Most of Aristotle's writings have been preserved. Andronicus, who published an edition of Aristotle's works between 60 and 50 B.C., places the number of his books at 1000. The works published by Aristotle, however, existed only in fragments. His lectures to pupils which we have were intended only for that purpose and not for publication. Aristotle's dialogues are not available, but his lectures are.

Aristotle's classification of the various branches of knowledge obtains to this day. Before his designation, all knowledge was considered within the province of philosophy. He classified his subject-matter with such logical precision that even today his divisions make sense.

Aristotle's Problem

Aristotle began by reconsidering some fundamental assumptions of Plato. Plato had placed the eternal forms beyond the stars in order to separate them from the actual world of experience. He referred to the world of sense as mere appearance. But here Aristotle was dissatisfied: matter required a more precise and satisfactory explanation. The gap between form and matter had to be bridged. How could the changeless ideas impact a lifeless irrational substratum? Plato seemed to have resorted to mythology and popular religion as he treated the Demiurge and the world-soul. Was this based upon ignorance instead of knowledge? The radical dualism of ideas and things was a serious concern for Aristotle as he considered Plato's system. How could this be overcome?

Aristotle engaged these issues directly. He retained the changeless eternal ideas, but denied their transcendent status. He brought them down from heaven to earth, so to speak. Forms are not apart from things, but inherent in them. They are not transcendent, but immanent. Matter is not to be equated with non-being. Form and matter are not separate—they are eternally together. Matter combines with form to constitute individual things. Each individual thing moves, changes, grows and evolves under the direction of its form. The sense world is more than an imitation of the real world—it *is* the real world. Form and matter come together and are the true object of science. Aristotle conceived the domain of science in this realistic fashion. Aristotle was at home in natural science. He studied it and encouraged the advancement of natural science. His perspective made provisions for physics as well as metaphysics, to provide an example of his broad interests.

Aristotelian Logic

The creation of the science of logic is one of the great achievements of Aristotle. This intellectual feat is without parallel in Western thought. It is true that logic was anticipated before Aristotle. We may recall, for example, the dialectical arguments of Zeno, the subtleties of the Sophists, the Socratic definitions of concepts, the Platonic dialectic, etc. But Aristotle alone is responsible for a systematic formulation of the principles of reasoning. His logic has dominated Western thought. There have been only a few revolts against his system of logic. I shall mention just two: first, that of Francis Bacon, who advocated the inductive method instead of the deductive; second, that of Bertrand Russell, who advocated a mathematical approach to logic. Thus the logic of Aristotle has reigned for more than two thousand years.

Logic holds a central place in the thought of Aristotle. It precedes other forms of knowledge. Logic, according to Aristotle, is the "science of sciences." It is the indispensable precondition for all science. It is the tool of scientific research, to be applied to every sphere of knowledge.

Logic is the science of correct thinking. Scientific thought is measured by strict necessity—a thing must be something which cannot be something else. That is to say, in order to establish a scientific proposition one must do two things. First, one must show that such and such has been the case. Second, one must establish that it could not possibly be otherwise.

For example, an arithmetical proposition such as "two plus three equals five" is an archetype of all scientific truth. It is inconceivable that it could be otherwise. On the other hand, the statement that swans are white or that fire produces heat could possibly be untrue. The latter cases are said to be accidental or contingent judgments. Thinking consists in reasoning, or scientific demonstration, in deriving the particular from the universal, the conditioned from its causes. *Inferences* are composed of *judgments* which, when expressed in language, are called *propositions*. Judgments consist of *concepts*, which are expressed in *terms*. Aristotle is mainly concerned with judgments or propositions. Aristotle discusses the nature and different kinds of judgments, the various relations in which they stand to one another and different types of demonstration.

Aristotle seeks to find in other sciences the demonstrative certainty of mathematics. This is possible only through syllogisms in which conclusions are based upon premises which, in turn, are the conclusions of other premises. But this process cannot go on indefinitely. We must finally reach propositions which cannot be proved deductively, but which, nevertheless, are absolutely certain. Scientific knowledge rests upon basic truths or axioms which neither admit or require proof.

A basic truth is one which has no proposition prior to it. Such truths are the first links in the long chain of reasoning. Basic truths are known by intuition—immediate or direct insight of reason. Intuition is the apprehension of the universal element in the particular. Since intuition departs from the apprehension of the particular, Aristotle refers to this process as induction. For instance, reason assures us that the whole is greater than its parts. Here we have a direct or intuitively self-evident principle like those in mathematics. Each science, according to Aristotle, has such self-evident principles. This is especially true of metaphysics.

Demonstration is the process of elaborating the derivative propositions from the original truths. Deduction takes the form of a syllogism or a series of syllogisms. A syllogism is a foundational form of thought. It is a discourse in which from certain propositions (premises) something new (the conclusion) necessarily follows. A syllogism consists of two premises (*major* and *minor*) and a *conclusion*. A familiar example is as follows:

"All men are mortal" (major)
"Socrates is a man" (minor)
"Socrates is mortal" (conclusion).

A syllogism is a form of deductive reasoning. In it the particular is derived from the universal. Scientific demonstration is, therefore, syllogistic or deductive reasoning. The conclusion must follow necessarily from the premises. And the premises themselves must be universal and necessary—they must be proved to be grounded on other premises. The goal of knowledge is complete demonstration. The science of Aristotle's day was mathematics. This explains in part the importance of demonstration in logic.

Basic truth is inherent in reason itself. It stems from the direct intuition of reason. Intuition is essential to induction or the process whereby thought arises from sense perception. It moves from the perception of individual things to general principles or the knowledge of universals. Human reason, the highest part of the soul, has the power of discerning the forms in their particular expressions. These forms are the essences of things. They are real and are the principles of reason. That is to say, they are at once forms of thought and reality. Thought and being coincide.

Furthermore, basic truths are potential in the mind, but experience is needed to make reason aware of them as well as to bring them to the level of awareness. At this point, Aristotle comes close to Plato's theory of reminiscence. He insists that rational knowledge is implicit in the mind and is made explicit by experience. Our knowledge begins with sense perception. It rises from particular facts to universal concepts. It moves from "that which is better known to us" to "that which is better known and more certain in itself." Universals are the last things we reach in our thinking, but are first in nature. They are the first principles of reality.

Induction prepares us for deduction. The ideal of science is to derive particulars from universals, to furnish demonstration or necessary proof. This depends upon induction completing its work — that is, until experience has aroused the knowledge of the universal which lies dormant in our reason.

Aristotle in this way assigns experience and reason their different functions in knowledge and reconciles empiricism and rationalism. Knowledge is impossible without experience. And yet certain knowledge does not come from experience alone. Experience yields probable knowledge; while certain knowledge has a rational or *a priori* basis. In sum, Aristotle's logic concludes that genuine scientific knowledge is a body of necessary truths, some of which are basic and assured by intuition; the rest are syllogistically deduced.

Under Aristotle's logic, we need to examine his *categories*. These are the fundamental and indivisible concepts of thought. They are likewise basic features of the real. It is not possible to think of any real or existent thing except as subsumed under one or more of the categories. Categories are different kinds of being, and not mere subjective concepts.

Substance is pre-eminent among the categories. It is ultimate and independent of all other things. Other things depend on substance.

Categories are the most fundamental and universal predicates which can be affirmed of anything. Aristotle defines ten categories as follows. We can say

1. *What* a thing it is (i.e. man, *substance*).
2. How a thing is *constituted* (i.e. blue, *quality*).
3. How *large* it is (i.e. two feet, *quantity*).
4. How *related* (i.e. greater, *relation*).
5. Where it is *located* (i.e. in the room, *space*).
6. When it *happened* (i.e. today, *time*).
7. What *posture* it assumes (i.e. lies, *position*).
8. The *condition* it is in (i.e. armed, *state*).
9. What it *does* (i.e. burns, *activity*).
10. What it *suffers* (i.e. is burned, *passivity*).

Aristotle is saying that the objects of our experience exist in time and place, can be measured or counted, are related to other things, act and are acted upon, have essential and accidental qualities, etc. According to him, categories are more than forms of thought; they are also predicates of reality. A particular perceivable substance is the bearer of all of these categories, that of which they are predicated. The category of substance is all-important; for other categories exist in so far as they can be predicated of substance. Science, therefore, deals with the category of being, essence or substance which is the essential constitution of things.

Aristotle agreed with Parmenides that being and thought are inseparable. That is to say, whatever can be thought must be and whatever is can be thought. Logic comes in as the process whereby thought is measured and expressed. Our thinking must agree with logic if it is to achieve certain truth. In Aristotle the way from logic to metaphysics is direct. A theory of knowledge implies a theory of being. Notice the anticipation of Anselm's ontological argument in Aristotle.

Metaphysics

Metaphysics is concerned with being as being. According to Aristotle, being is not *Idea* but *substance* or *ousia*. Other categories are secondary to substance and exist only in relation to it. For example, a *quality* can exist only in a substance. Substance, on the other hand, exists in its own right.

Substance is an individual thing. The fundamental meaning of substance is that it is concrete and individual. Universals for Aristotle are not, as for Plato, self-subsistent things with an existence of their own. According to Aristotle, universals exist only in or through individual things.

Aristotle's critique of Plato is instructive of his own viewpoint. First, Aristotle rejects Plato's argument that Forms are required to make scientific knowledge possible. Knowledge of universals is necessary for science, but this proves only that universals exist. It does not establish that they exist independently of individual things. In fact, the Forms of Plato do not yield knowledge of individual things, since they are not in them as their essence. Second, Forms cannot account for motion or change, since they are without motion themselves. Objects are copies of them, and would appear also to be motionless. What is the source of motion? Plato had asserted that Forms are not the cause of motion, but went on to explain motion as arising from the activity of souls. Third, Aristotle insists that if Forms contain the essence of sensible objects, they cannot exist without such objects. The assumption that they do, makes it impossible to explain the relation of Forms to particular objects which exemplify them. Thus Plato does not adequately explain such relation by using terms like "participation" and "imitation." To say that Forms are patterns and other things share in them is to use empty words and poetical metaphors.

All these criticisms Aristotle directed against the transcendent character of the Platonic Forms and the contrast between *being* and *becoming*. Universals, according to Aristotle, exist only as characteristics of individual substances. Universals are real in the sense that there is an objective foundation for them in individual substances. But they are immanent in and not transcendent to things. The form of a person operates in bringing into existence at birth an individual person. The form of the person is embodied in the parent of the person. Aristotle seeks to do two things here. First, he seeks to bridge the world of Being and the world of Becoming. Second, he attempts to explain the change which occurs in the sensible world. His focus, therefore, is upon the world of becoming, of nature and its changes. His convictions point in the direction of *naturalism* and/or *empiricism*. This is to be contrasted with *idealism* in Plato.

An analysis of the sensible and changeable substances of nature indicates that each of them is composed of *form* and *matter*. The form, *eidos*, of a substance is not one component among others. It is, rather, the essence, *ousia* or structure, of the thing. It is that which constitutes it the kind of thing it is. Matter, on the other hand, is its substratum—that through which the form is realized. Since the form of a species is identical in all the members of a species, it is the matter which is its principle of individuation. That is to say, matter is that which marks off one member of the species from another. And yet, for Aristotle, there are supersensible and unchangeable substances as well as material and sensible ones. The highest of these is pure form without matter of any kind.

The world is a hierarchy of substances of various kinds. "Prime matter," or matter unrelated to form, does not exist. At the bottom of the scale of substances are the elements of earth, i.e. water, air and fire. These provide the matter out of which minerals and tissues of plants and animals are formed. These, in turn, furnish the matter for other parts of plants and animals, i.e. organs, and organs are the matter of which the body is composed. Above plants and animals is man. Man is the highest form of animal life. The human intellect is the highest aspect—it is corporeal and immortal. Still higher are intelligences which move the spheres. They are pure substances without bodies. God is at the top of the hierarchy as pure form without matter. Each substance has a definite place on the scale of being which ascends from inanimate to pure form.

Figure I
The Hierarchy of Reality
God—pure form without matter
Intelligences—without bodies (move spheres
from without)
Humans—(intellect, incorporeal, immortal)
Body—animals, plants, organs
Minerals (and tissue of animals and plants)
Simple Bodies (i.e. earth, water, air, fire)
(provide matter)

Aristotle is especially interested in the dynamic aspect of sensible substance, the change by which it passes from one state to another.

Substance A passes from the *potentiality* of B to the *actuality* of B through a process of *change*. He distinguishes between potentiality or *dynamis* and actuality (*entelecheia*). For example, an oak passes from a state of potentiality in an acorn to a state of actuality in a fully-grown tree. In like manner, the will of a person changes from the potentiality to the actuality of moral virtue. Change is not catastrophic but purposeful. It is not the case that A is sheerly not B and suddenly becomes B. If we consider A more carefully, we will find some of the conditions of B-ness already present. If this were not so, A would never become B. The point can be illustrated in this manner. A person who builds houses can do so if a decision is made. On the other hand, one who has not learned the art of building cannot do so without instruction. Once the skill has been acquired, the potential leading to the actual is inherent in the potential. A cannot pass from potentiality to actuality without the agency of something which is already actual. Hence actuality is prior to potentiality and potentiality is based upon actuality.

Matter is the principle of potentiality, and form is the principle of actuality. Only formless matter which we can think, but does not exist as such, is pure potentiality. Concrete matter always has form and is, in a sense, actual. In order to explain our world of change, we must assume form and matter. Every form is, like a Platonic idea, eternal, but instead of being *outside* matter, it is *in* matter. Form and matter have always co-existed; they are co-eternal principles of things. Form realizes itself in the thing; it causes the thing to move and to realize an *end* or *purpose*. The cooperation of form and matter which is discernible in the process of nature is even more clearly illustrated in the creative activity of humans. An artist in producing a work of art has an idea or plan in mind. The artist acts on matter through the motion of the hands, being governed by a plan, to realize a purpose. This developmental process described in terms of the antithesis of potential and actual, of form and matter, is governed by *causes*.

Cause for Aristotle was broader than its meaning in modern science. Cause for Aristotle designates any condition requisite to the occurrence of something. The general term Aristotle uses for cause is *aitia*. He distinguishes four causes which explain change: material, efficient, formal and final.

Before discussing the *causes*, we need to indicate how closely *physics* and *metaphysics* are related in Aristotle. Physics deals with substances which are changeable. It analyzes the nature common to all natural bodies, animate and inanimate, which have in themselves a source of movement and rest. It is concerned with both matter and the form of these bodies, and with the causes in them. They are distinguished from artificial bodies such as beds or garments by the fact that there is no inherent principle of change in the latter. In contrast, metaphysics analyzes being as such, concerns itself with unchangeable substances as well as changeable ones, and culminates in theology which deals with God, the transcendent and immaterial First Cause, to which we will come later.

This distinction between inanimate and animate, between unchangeable substances and changeable ones is important in the explication of the four causes.

The four causes are explained in the following manner:

1. The *material* cause is that from which (Greek *ex hou*) a thing is made. This was the cause which Thales had in mind when he referred to the material substratum of a thing, i.e. the formless bronze out of which the artist will fashion a stature.

2. The *formal* cause is the essence (*to eidos*), the pattern or structure which is to become embodied in a thing when it is fully realized. It is that which the thing really is. In the case of a builder, it would be the plan or blueprint.

3. The *efficient* cause (*to hothen he kinesis*) is the moving cause. It is the active agent which produces the thing as its effect. It is that through which the thing is produced. Examples would be a carpenter who builds a house or an artist who paints a picture.

4. The *final* cause (*to hou heneka*) is the end or purpose for which something exists. For example, a house is built to dwell in.

In sum, the material cause of a house is the stone or wood out of which it is built. The formal cause is the plan which first exists in the human mind and then is realized in the structure. The efficient cause is the builder, by whose agency the house is constructed. The final cause is the purpose for which it is built, e.g. habitation. We should observe, however, that the efficient cause is not necessarily eternal to this. If the efficient cause is in a house it is one thing, but in a horse, the case is quite different. The final cause is actually the controlling cause. Without purpose or end, the process is futile or perhaps does not begin at all.

Aristotle's causes may be seen in opposition to a pure mechanistic explanation of causation. He offers an argument against the materialists who oppose final causes and attempt to explain all changes by necessity (*ananke*). He advocates purpose or teleology rather than chance as a governing factor in nature. Nature usually acts in a certain way if unobstructed. Natural process is directed toward an end that is to be realized, each stage leads to the next. In art and in nature there is a relation between the antecedent and the consequent. Aristotle studied the behavior of animals and the growth of plants to establish this point. For example, swallows make a nest, spiders spin a web and plants yield fruit. The adaptations of plants and animals provide empirical evidence for the view that final causes are operative not merely in humans but below this level as well. He perceived, however, that nature sometimes fails to obtain her ends. These oddities are due to chance. They are by nature, but not according to nature. These are exceptions and not the rule, so to speak.

This teleological understanding of nature is not original in Aristotle. It is present in Anaxagoras, Socrates and Plato. Plato makes use of a world-soul and Anaxagoras speaks of *nous*. Aristotle is not willing to accept these explanations. He speaks, instead, as if there were some teleological activity inherent in nature. Aristotle does speak *ho theos*, but does not provide a satisfactory treatment of the relation between nature and God. What he says about God would appear to preclude any purposive activity in nature on the part of God. His teleology is "unconscious"—it implies a purpose which is not the purpose of mind. Is this really purpose?

Nature consists of a plurality of individual substances in which different forms immanent in matter are realized by passing from potentiality to actuality through the process of change. It is through this process that final causes are unconsciously aimed at and normally attained. But the process in each case requires an efficient cause to set it in motion. Since actuality is prior to potentiality, this moving cause must be actual. In addition to the proximate moving cause, there must be an ultimate or first moving cause. There is that which as first of all things moves all things. The first moving cause or Prime Mover is the culmination of Aristotle's metaphysics and his major contribution to theology.

Aristotle's proof for the existence of the Prime Mover is found in his *Metaphysics*, Book XII. This constitutes his cosmological argument for God as the First Cause of all change in the world. Everything depends upon substances. If all substances are perishable, all things would be perishable. But there are two things which must always have existed and can never cease to be. These are *movement* and *time*. There could be no *before* and *after* if time ceased to exist. Movement, like time, must be continuous, since time is the same as movement or an attribute of it. The only continuous movement is movement in space, and the only continuous movement in space is circular. Aristotle argues in Book VII of *Physics* that things do not turn back—all motion is single and continuous. Continuous motion is circular—there must be an *external circular motion*.

What is the cause of this motion? An eternal motion must be produced by an eternal substance which is capable of moving things. This substance must also exercise its capacity as a mover so that its essence must be activity. Otherwise, it would be possible for it not to exercise its capacity as a mover and motion would not be necessary and eternal. But its very essence is actuality; being eternal it is also immaterial. Matter, on the other hand, is potentiality and involved in change, and as such cannot be eternal. Aristotle concludes as follows: There must exist an eternal substance, the essence of which is actuality. It is immaterial and imparts the perpetual motion upon which all motion and change depend.

We will leave Aristotle at this point, but out of necessity will need to return to his profound contribution to Western thought again and again. His most profound contribution to Christian theology is reflected in the thought of Aquinas.

IV

Athens to Alexandria

The title of this chapter may not be exact, but it does represent the coverage of the subject-matter to be discussed. What I have in mind is the development of philosophy after Aristotle in the Greco-Roman context. We will focus on major thought movements and representative thinkers. My controlling purpose is to show how the development of philosophy influenced both Jewish and Christian thought.

Along the way we will encounter Stoicism, Epicureanism, Neo-Pythagoreanism, Middle Platonism and Neo-Platonism. This stream of thought-development eventually impacts upon such religious thinkers as Philo, Origen and later Augustine. Since my purpose is to show how philosophy has been the interpretative means by which theology has expressed itself through intellection, my intention will become evident as we proceed.

Stoicism[1]

According to the Stoics, only the individual exists. They rejected Plato's transcendental universal. Aristotle's concrete universal was also set aside. The Stoic founded knowledge on sense-perception. The soul is originally a *tabla rasa*, and, in order for it to know, there must be perception.

Even though the Stoics were Empiricists, they were also advocates of reason. Reason was conceived as the product of human development, but they also believed in general ideas, apparently antecedent to experience. We have a natural predisposition to form general ideas—they are in some sense innate. It is only through reason that reality can be known. However, the place of reason among the Stoics is to be seen in relation to their concern for the criterion of truth. The Stoics assert that the criterion for truth lies in the perception itself—that is, in the perception that compels the assent of the soul.

The Stoic cosmology consists of two principles of reality—active and passive. The two principles are material and together form one whole. Their cosmology was a monistic materialism. Some inconsistency is notable in this position. The passive principle is devoid of qualities, while the active principle is immanent Reason or God. Finality in the universe points to God or Providence. Everything has been arranged for the good of humans. Humans are the highest phenomena in the universe. Humans possess consciousness. Since the whole cannot be less than its parts, the whole world must be conscious. God, therefore, is the consciousness of the world.

Like Heraclitus, the Stoics make fire the stuff of all things. God is the active fire which is immanent in the universe. God is the primal source. Everything exists in God or states of God. For example, God is related to the world as soul to body, being the soul of the world.

Heraclitus did not work out a doctrine of universal conflagration—whereby the world returns to the primeval fire. The Stoics, however, added this doctrine. God forms the world and then takes it back into himself. There follows an unending series of world constructions and destructions. This is associated with the belief that each human returns in identical manner in each successive world. Nietzsche's "Eternal Recurrence" is descriptive of this notion. Any meaningful understanding of human freedom appears to be absent.

Freedom of will implies doing with conscious assent what one will do automatically. A reign of necessity is expressed in the concept of Fate. Fate, however, is not different from God, Providence or universal reason which orders all things for the best. Fate and Providence are but different aspects of God. But this rigid determinism is modified by the Stoic insistence on "interior freedom." A person can alter his/her judgment on events and attitude towards events by seeing or welcoming them as an expression of God's will. In this sense only, humans are free.

The Stoic held that God orders all things for the best. This is contradicted (apparently so by experience). They needed, therefore, to bring the evil in the world into harmony with their optimism. So Chrysippus sought to formulate a theodicy to satisfy this challenge. He argued that the imperfection of individuals subserves the perfection of the whole. There is no evil if things are looked at *sub specie aeternitatis*. Furthermore, Chrysippus argued that goods could not have existed without evil. In treating a pair of contraries, we find them interdependent—one cannot exist without the other. For example, the pain of hunger moves one to partake of food, which provides nourishment, which fosters good health.

But what about moral evil? According to the Stoics no act is evil in itself. It is the "intention" or the moral condition of the agent that makes the act evil—the act as a physical entity is neutral (amoral). Moral evil cannot be a positive entity, the Stoics argued. The world order is consistent with the Creator which is the source of all goodness. Moral evil is, therefore, a privation of right order in the human will. It is out of harmony with right reason. Here as elsewhere we note that ideas have consequences. The impact of Chrysippus's reflections on evil, especially moral evil, appears in Augustine, Leibnitz and elsewhere.

Philosophy for the Stoics was a science of conduct. The end of life, happiness, consists in virtue. The natural life is life according to nature—the agreement of human action with the law of nature or the harmony of the human will with the divine will. The Stoic maxim "live according to nature" sums up this outlook. The universe is governed by the law of nature. Nature is approached from an anthropological viewpoint. To conform to one's essential nature and to live according to reason are the same thing, since the universe is governed by the law of nature. Animals live by instinct, which points to self-preservation. Humans, on the other hand, are endowed with reason, which gives them superiority over animals. To live a life of virtue means more than following one's own nature. It means following the nature of the universe. One lives a life which corresponds to right reason.

The cardinal virtues are designed as moral insight. They are courage, self-control, temperance, and justice. These virtues stand or fall together. One who possesses one possesses all. Virtues, all together, are the basis for one's character. Conversely, vices represent an undesirable character. A wise person lives a virtuous life and fulfills his/her duty. This strict moralism characterized earlier Stoicism. Later, however, more latitude was provided for becoming wise and virtuous. One's life was evaluated more in terms of progress. Character, therefore, is measured more in terms of progressing toward virtue or wisdom.

As to passions and affections, these were undesirable. Pleasure, sorrow, depression, desire and fear were regarded as unnatural as well as irrational. One should eliminate these and acquire a state of Apathy. Apathy leads to a state of moral freedom. One who obtains a condition of indifference to affections acquires complete independence of externals. Only thus may one be morally free.

Cosmopolitanism was one of the greatest affirmations of the Stoic ethic. We are naturally social beings. Reason dictates that we live in society. Reason is likewise the common essential nature of all humans. There is one law for all and one human family. Therefore, the Stoics insisted that divisions of humankind into warring states is absurd. The wise person is the citizen of the world. All have a claim to our good will. Even our enemies deserve the right to our mercy and forgiveness. All this begins in self-love. But it extends beyond individual self-love and eventually embraces family, friends, fellow citizens and, finally, the whole of humanity. In sum, the Stoic ethical ideal is reached when we love all humans as we love ourselves — when our self-love embraces all that is connected with self, including humanity at large, with equal intensity.

Epicureanism

We turn now to Epicureanism, established by Epicurus, who was born at Samos in 342 B.C. He was introduced to the thought of Democritus as a student. Epicurus came to Athens for military service at the age of eighteen. He later studied at Colophon, but returned to Athens to found his school. This school was instituted in his own garden. His house and garden were bequeathed to his disciples, who were devoted to him, even after his death. His pupils were required to memorize his teachings. There arose about Epicurus a cult of him as founder. This explains the philosophic orthodoxy which remained for some time among his followers.

A Latin poet, T. Lucretius Carus (91–51 B.C.) expressed the Epicurean philosophy in his poem *De Rerum Natura*. He asserted that the main purpose of this philosophy was to liberate humans from the fear of the gods and of death and provide peace of soul for them.

Logic was important to Epicurus in so far as it provided a criterion for truth. Dialectics interested him only as it directly subserved physics. But physics again was of concern only as it served ethics. He had little interest in scientific pursuits and found mathematics useless. His focus was upon the conduct of life. Epicurus was preoccupied with sense-knowledge. For him the fundamental criterion of truth was perception. Perception takes place when images of objects penetrate the sense organs. Epicureans included under perception imaginative representations, all perception taking place through the reception of images. When these images flow constantly from the same object and enter by the sense organs, we observe perception in a narrow sense. On the other hand, when individual images enter through the pores of the body, they are mixed up, and imaginative pictures arise. We are able to determine error only through judgment. If we judge that an image corresponds to an external object and it does not, we are in error. Unfortunately, Epicurus does not assist us in determining the correspondence of the image to its external object. Perception remains, however, the fundamental criterion for truth.

Concepts are a second criterion. A concept is defined as a memory image. After we have had perception of an object, the memory image or general image of the object follows as we make sense contact with the object. Opinion or judgment must be confirmed by experience. Even hidden or unperceived causes must not contradict experience.

Feelings in reference to conduct are a third criterion. Thus the feeling of pleasure is the criterion for what we should choose, while the feeling of pain indicates what is to be avoided. Hence, Epicurus asserted that the criteria of truth are the senses, the perceptions and the passions.

We recall that Epicurus chose his physical theory to undergird his ethical concerns. He desired to free humans from the fear of the gods and the future life and give them peace of soul. Epicurus did not deny the existence of the gods. What he attempted to demonstrate was that they do not interfere in human affairs. There is no reason for worship, sacrifices or devotion to gods. By rejecting immortality he sought to free humans of the fear of death. He described death as mere extinction, or the absence of all consciousness and feeling. In death there is no judgment, and no punishment awaits one in the future life. Death, he asserts, is nothing to us, for it is devoid of sensation. Epicurus used the thought of Democritus to argue his points. The atomistic materialism of Democritus served his end. Democritus had explained all phenomena by mechanical motions of atoms. Because the soul as well as the body is composed of atoms, the basis for divine intervention, as well as the immortality of the soul, is ruled out.

The bodies of our experience are composed of pre-existing material entities or atoms. These atoms resolve into the entities of which they are composed. The ultimate constituents of the universe are therefore atoms. Death is but the privation of perception. At death the atoms of the soul are separated, and there can be no more perception.

The world exists by means of mechanical causes and there is no place for teleology. Here Epicureans rejected outright the anthropocentric teleology of the Stoics. They saw evil as in irreconcilable conflict with any notion of providence. The Epicureans conceived of the gods as being happy, indifferent to human affairs, drinking, and speaking Greek. The gods embody the tranquility of the ethical ideal. They were conceived in anthropomorphic terms for this purpose. The knowledge we have of their happy condition comes through reason. True piety consists of right thought. A wise person does not fear death, for it is mere extinction. Neither is he fearful of the gods, for they are unconcerned with human affairs and exact no retribution.

We now come to the heart of Epicurus' philosophical outlook, his understanding of *pleasure*. Like the Cyrenaics, Epicurus made pleasure the end of life. He asserted that every being strives after pleasure and that happiness consists in obtaining pleasure. But what does he mean by pleasure?

Epicurus was not concerned about the pleasures of the moment or individual sensations. He was preoccupied with those pleasures that endure for a lifetime. Again, pleasure was more related to the absence of pain than to positive satisfaction. Pleasure is manifested, pre-eminently, in serenity of soul. While the presence of pleasure brings with it health of body, Epicurus emphasized intellectual pleasure. It is the permanence of pleasure he is seeking, together with the absence of pain. He does not associate differences in pleasure with differences of moral value. His ultimate goal is health of body and tranquillity of soul. Epicurus, therefore, did not advocate libertinism or excess, but a calm and tranquil life blessed by reason.

It would appear that principles dismissed through the front door return through the back door. Epicurean ethics lead to a moderate asceticism, self-control and independence. Virtue is a means to tranquility of soul. Its value is estimated, however, by its power to produce pleasure. Virtues such as simplicity, moderation, temperance, cheerfulness are conducive to pleasure. This is not true of unrestrained luxury or insatiable ambition. A just person is free from disquietude, while injustice leads to guilt and fear of punishment. To be happy one must live in such a way as to have nothing to fear from others. Epicurus appears sounder, to us, in his moral practice than he does in the theoretical foundations of his ethic.

In order to live pleasantly, one must live prudently, honorably and justly. One cannot live in an agreeable manner without keeping these virtues. One who is virtuous is not so much one who is enjoying pleasure, but one who conducts life in the search for pleasure. Virtue is necessary for lasting happiness.

Friendship is very important to Epicurus. This emphasis on friendship is based on egoistic considerations. One cannot live a tranquil life without friendship, and yet friendship gives pleasure. Epicurus goes on to assert that an unselfish affection arises during friendship and eventually one loves the friend as one does oneself. The egoistic aspect arises as Epicurus denounces politics. Friendship fits into his social theory, but politics is against tranquillity of soul.

When this is compared with the earlier outlook of the Cyrenaics, some interesting facts emerge. The Cyrenaics emphasized positive pleasures; the Epicureans stressed the negative side, calm and tranquillity. The Cyrenaics considered bodily suffering worse than mental suffering, while the Epicureans considered mental suffering worse than bodily suffering. For example, the soul can recall past suffering as well as anticipate future suffering. In sum, much of Cyrenaicism is absorbed into Epicureanism, but there are important differences.

Finally, it is important to make some distinction between Epicurus and the movement as it developed. This is not a philosophy for moral heroes. But, in its original intention, it was not intended to sponsor base living. It is, therefore, very important to consider the thought and life of Epicurus in their temporal and thought context.

Our next encounter is with Middle Platonism. A brief explication of the reflection of this period will set the stage for a better understanding of Neo-Platonism. This is of great consequence because of the importance of this developing tradition in the Jewish and Christian theologies to follow.

Plato did not leave lectures. His followers, therefore, did not have in their possession a systematized philosophic deposit. The popular dialogues did not provide the basis for a rigid orthodoxy. It is not surprising that Middle Platonism has eclecticism as its main characteristic. Again, Middle Platonism resembled Neo-Pythagoreanism in its insistence upon divine transcendence, intermediary beings and mysticism.

Middle Platonism

Middle Platonism paid avid attention to the study of Plato's dialogues. This led to a deep reverence for Plato. Beyond this, the Middle Platonists stressed the differences between Plato's thought and other philosophical systems. Many tracts were written against the Peripatetics (the Aristotelians) and the Stoics. This movement was not, however, unified. Middle Platonism was a transition-stage with many different points of view.

Plutarch of Chaeronea is a notable representative of Middle Platonism. I use his thought as an example. He was born in A.D. 45 and was educated at Athens. He visited Rome often and met many outstanding personages there. He befriended these notables, and wrote his famous *Lives* as a result.

Plutarch's thought was decidedly eclectic. He was influenced not only by Plato but by the Peripatetics, the Stoics, and the Neo-Pythagoreans as well. He had a distrustful attitude toward theoretical speculation, and made room in his thought for prophecy, revelation and enthusiasm as he sought a purer conception of the Deity. He speaks of an immediate intuition or contact with the Transcendental. He thus helped to prepare the way for the Plotinian (from Plotinus) doctrine of ecstasy.

He aimed at a purer conception of God, as we have noted. This led him to make several important assertions. He insists that we can have no intercourse with God while we are here below and are encumbered by bodily affections. Through philosophical thought we may only faintly touch God, as in a dream. When our souls are released from the body, we will have the fulfillment of our desire to behold God as pure, invisible and changeless. God, according to Plutarch, is not the author of evil. He found the source of evil elsewhere, in the World-Soul. The World-Soul as the cause of evil is set over against God as the pure Good. Hence a dualism is asserted of these two principles, good and bad. This dualism is maintained, but there is some ambiguity in Plutarch's explanation of it. The evil principle seems to have become the divine World-Soul at creation by participation with reason, which emanates from God. The World-Soul is not destitute of reason and harmony, but it continues, at the same time, to act as the evil principle. In this way his dualism is sustained.

According to Plutarch, God is not responsible for evil and is elevated above the world. It is, therefore, essential to introduce intermediary beings below God. Plutarch accepted the gods of Xenocrates (or demons) as the bridge between God and humanity. Some of these are more akin to God, others are tainted by the evil of the lower world. The good demons are the instruments of providence. Plutarch was a foe to superstition or anything unworthy of God, but he expressed sympathy for popular religion. He insists that the various religions of humankind worship the same God under different names. He used allegorical interpretation, in order to justify popular beliefs. For example, Osiris represents the good principle, while Tryphon stands for the bad principle. Isis points to matter which to Plutarch is neutral. Matter, however, has a natural tendency and love for the Good. In this latter opinion, he sits loose to Plato.

Plutarch asserts a dualism between spirit and matter — this relates to the body-soul dualism of his psychology. The dualism between spirit and matter is superimposed upon the soul-body dualism as follows. Just as the soul is better and more divine than the body, so is spirit better and more divine than matter. The latter is subject to passions, the former is the "demon" in the human which should rule. Plutarch affirms immortality as he describes the happiness of the future life as one experiences reunion with relatives and friends.

In ethics, Plutarch is influenced by the Peripatetics and Stoics. When he emphasizes the need to attain the mean between excess and defect, he is Peripatetic. He follows the Stoics, on the other hand, in permitting suicide and in his espousal of cosmopolitanism. His Roman experience and his acceptance of the emperor as God's representative is reflective of Stoic passivity in the realm of politics.

As to the cosmology of Plutarch, he believed that the world was created in time. Furthermore, this necessitates that the soul has priority over the body. God has priority over the world also.

As I observed at the outset of this discussion on Middle Platonism, we have here an anticipation of Neo-Platonism, which is so essential to the understanding of Jewish and Christian theology. This is especially true of the Hellenization process in Alexandria. We turn now to Neo-Platonism.[2]

Plotinus and Neo-Platonism

Plotinus was born in Egypt about A.D. 203. He studied under several professors, but was not pleased with any of his teachers until he met Ammonius Saccas at age twenty-eight. He remained a pupil of Ammonius until 242, when he joined the Persian expedition of the Emperor Gordian. He was interested in studying Persian philosophy. The expedition was aborted because of the assassination of the emperor. Plotinus arrived in Rome aged forty. There he was befriended by high officials including the Emperor Gallienus and his wife. He even anticipated the founding of a city, Platonopolis, as a concrete realization of Plato's Republic. At first he had consent from the emperor. Later the emperor withdrew his consent and the plan fell through.

The writing style of Plotinus was very complicated, though he had an eloquent oral style. In his latter years his weak eyesight prevented him from correcting his manuscripts. Fortunately a celebrated pupil, Porphyry, wrote the life of Plotinus and attempted to arrange his writings in systematic form. Porphyry arranged the writings of Plotinus into six books, each of which contained nine chapters. Hence the name *Enneads* (nines) was applied to them.

At Rome, Plotinus was advisor to persons in authority. He became a kind of spiritual director. He was a gentle and affectionate person. His personal life was ascetic. Yet he expressed his kindness in several ways. One example was that he took orphan children into his house and acted as their guardian. He led a deep spiritual life. Porphyry met his teacher during Plotinus's sixtieth year. Porphyry relates that his master experienced ecstatic union with God four times in the six years in which he was his disciple. Plotinus died about A.D. 269. His last words to his attending physician were these: "I was waiting for you, before that which is divine in me departs to unite itself with the Divine in the universe."[3]

God, according to Plotinus, is absolutely transcendent. He is the One, beyond all thought and all being, ineffable and incomprehensible.[4] The One cannot be identical with the sum of individual things, for it is these individual things which required a Source or Principle, and this Principle must be distinct from them and logically prior to them. The One of Plotinus is closely related to the transcent in Neo-Pythagoreanism and Middle Platonism rather than to the monistic principle of Parmenides. Plotinus sets the One above being. This does not mean that the One is non-existent. It means that the One transcends all being of which we have experience. The concept of being is drawn from the objects of our experience, but the One is above all those objects and as a result also transcends the concepts based upon those objects.

Since God is one, without multiplicity or division, there can be in the One no duality of substance and accident. Plotinus, therefore, is unwilling to ascribe to God any positive accidents. If we say that the One is "this" or "not that," we delimit it and make it a particular thing. In reality, it is beyond all things and cannot be delimited by such predication. In spite of this reservation, Plotinus is willing to attribute Goodness to the One, if properly understood. Goodness is not an inherent quality of the One. Goodness implies that the One is Good and not that "goodness" is a quality or attributes of the One. The One is *The Good* rather than "good." Again, we may ascribe to the One neither thought, will nor activity. Thought implies a distinction between subject and object or the thinker and the thought. The same can be said of will and activity. For instance, there is a distinction between the agent and the object on which it acts. Plotinus insists, therefore, that the One is beyond all distinctions whatsoever. The One cannot distinguish himself from himself, and so is beyond self-consciousness. Only the predicates of unity and goodness may be ascribed to God (in the sense that God is the One and the Good). Even these predicates are inadequate and are used analogously (i.e. unity expresses the denial of plurality and goodness refers to the effect one thing has upon another). It would appear that what Plotinus aims at is really above thought or speech and beyond the range of usual human experience. What we understand is this: The One or God is beyond being, One, indivisible, unchanging, eternal, without past or future, a constant self-identity.

If we accept the non-being of God of Plotinus, how will we explain the multiplicity of finite things? God cannot limit himself to finite things, as though they were part of him, nor can he create the world by a free act of his will. This is so because creation is an activity, and we are not allowed to ascribe activity to God as an impairment of his unchangeability. In view of these problems, Plotinus has recourse to the metaphor of "emanation." While God remains untouched, undiminished and unmoved, the world issues from him. The world proceeds from God by necessity—there is a principle of necessity which determines that the less perfect should come from the more perfect. An example is the reflection of an object in a mirror. The object which is mirrored is reduplicated, yet the mirror itself does not undergo any change or loss.[5]

The question could be asked: Was Plotinus a pantheist? He rejects free creation *ex nihilo* and yet the One, as prior principle, remains undiminished by subordinate forms of existence. Plotinus does reject free creation out of nothing on the ground that this would imply change in God. But he equally rejects a pantheistic understanding of creation. God does not impart his being to individual creatures. Creation is not a self-emptying process on the part of God. Plotinus moves between theistic creation and a fully pantheistic monistic explanation. He does not opt for an ultimate dualism, but any notion that he is pantheistic requires careful qualifications.

Plotinus views the relation of God to the world in terms of emanations. We need, therefore, to look at the several stages of emanation to determine the manner of God's relation to the world. Emanation appears to refer to procession as described earlier. But it also seems to imply fecundity or "fruitfulness" of being in God, so that there is an "overflowingness" of the "beingness" of the One into the multiplicity of existent realities in the universe.

The first emanation from the One is Thought or Mind, *Nous*, which is intuition or immediate apprehension. Mind has a two-fold object: (*a*) the One, (*b*) itself. In *Nous* exist the Ideas, of classes and individuals—the whole multitude of Ideas is contained indivisibly in *Nous*. It is in *Nous*, therefore, that multiplicity first appears, since the One is elevated above all multiplicity. *Nous* is also eternal, beyond time. Its blessedness is not an acquired state but an eternal possession. *Nous* knows all things together in the eternal present.

Soul emanates from *Nous*. Soul corresponds to the World-Soul of Plato's *Timaeus*. The World-Soul is incorporeal and indivisible, but it provides a connecting link between the super-sensible and the sensible worlds. The Soul looks at once upwards to the *Nous* and downward to the world of nature. Whereas Plato deposited only one World-Soul, Plotinus has two, a higher and a lower. The higher one is near to *Nous* and has no immediate contact with material world. The lower World-Soul is the real soul of the phenomenal world. This second soul, Plotinus termed nature or *physis*. The phenomenal world owes all the reality it possessed to its participation in Ideas, which are in *Nous*. These Ideas do not operate in the sensible world and have no direct relation to it.

Individual human souls proceed from the World-Soul. They are divided into two elements with a third mediating element. There is a higher element which belongs to the sphere of *Nous*, and a lower element which is directly associated with the body. The soul, according to Plotinus, existed before its union with the body, which is represented by a fall. The soul survives the body, though without memory of earthly existence. A view of transmigration is also implied. Personal souls are gathered together in the World-Soul. There is likewise personal immortality, since the soul is real and nothing that is real will perish.

The material world is below the sphere of the soul. In keeping with his notion of the emanation process as radiation of light, Plotinus describes light as moving from the center and passing outward. It grows dimmer at a gradual pace. Finally it shades off into a total darkness which is matter-in-itself—conceived as the privation of light. Matter proceeds from the One (ultimately), in the sense that it becomes a factor in creation only through the process of emanation from the One. But matter, in itself (at its lowest limit), forms the bottom-most stage of the universe: it is the antithesis to the One. In so far as matter is illumined by form and enters into the composition of material objects, it is not complete darkness. But in so far as it stands opposite to the intelligible, it represents unilluminated darkness. Here Plotinus mixes Platonic and Aristotelian themes. He adopts Plato's conception of matter as the antithesis to the intelligible and the privation of light. But he also embraces Aristotle's notion of matter as the substrate of form, as an integral component of material objects. Matter is partially illuminated and does not exist separately in the concrete as complete darkness—the principle of non-being.

Plotinus goes beyond this fusion of Platonic and Aristotelian cosmological themes as he discusses the principle of evil. In this latter pursuit he shows Orphic and Neo-Pythagorean influence. Matter, at its lowest grade, devoid of quality, as unilluminated privation, is evil itself—it does not possess evil as an inherent quality, but rather stands over against the Good as its radical antithesis. It is at this juncture that Plotinus comes close to a dualism which is inconsistent with his system. It is to be remembered that he deposits evil as a negative principle. Plotinus does not, therefore, depreciate the visible universe—he affirms it. The tendency to depreciate the visible universe shows up in his psychology and ethics, but is offset in his cosmology, for he insists upon the unity and harmony of the cosmos. We find him opposing the Gnostic contempt for the world.

The universe is the work of the World-Soul. It is a unified and eternal reality, bound together by Divine Providence.

We need to consider Plotinus's psychology and ethics, in order to explain what he understands as ecstatic union with the One. In his psychology he assigns three parts of the individual soul. The highest of these (cf. the *Nous* of Aristotle) is uncontaminated by matter and remains rooted in the intelligible world. And yet in so far as the soul is united with the body, it is contaminated by matter. There follows the need for an ethical ascent with an ultimate goal of union with the One. During this ethical ascent, the ethical element is subservient to the intellectual element, as in Aristotle. The first stage consists of purification under the impulses of *Eros (cf. Plato's Symposium)*. This frees one from the domination of the body and the senses and leads one to the practice of the four cardinal virtues (courage, self-control, temperance and justice). Next, the soul must rise above sense-perception, turn toward *Nous* and be concerned with philosophy and science. A higher stage carries the soul beyond discursive thought to union with *Nous*. But all these stages are but preparatory to the final stage described as the mystical union with God or the One.

In this final stage there is the absence of all duality. In thought of God or about God the subject is separated from the object; but there is no such separation in ecstatic union. God is "outside" no one but is present to all, even they do not know it. This ecstatic union is of brief duration in so far as the present life is concerned. We look for its completion and its constant possession in the future state, when we are freed from the hinderance of the body. The life beyond the earthly pilgrimage is described as the "flight of the alone to the Alone."

Plotinus, as we have seen, based his conclusions upon personal experience as well as his own creative mind and past speculation. The centre of his thought is religion and mysticism. Philosophy passes into religion. His thought was the intellectual response to the contemporary quest for personal salvation. The thought of Plotinus was a rival to Christianity. But its lack of a sense of history, its complicated philosophical system as well as its lack of popular appeal, prevented it from being the rival it might have been. Christianity, on the other hand, has a rootage in history, popular appeal and a tendency toward speculation. It is not difficult to understand that Christianity and Neo-Platonism share much in common (i.e. in speculation, ethics and spirituality). It only remained necessary to have a giant theologian like Augustine discover this. In this way the philosophy of Plotinus became an intellectual means to interpret Christianity for the universal church.[6]

V

What Has Athens to do with Jerusalem?

The encounter between biblical revelation and Greek philosophy and culture is cross-disciplinary in character. That is to say, scholars dealing with Jewish and Christian scriptures, no less than historical theologians, must grapple with the cross-fertilization of ideas in the Greco-Roman period.

We must ask: What happened when a mainly philosophical humanistic rationalism encountered religions or revelation? Whatever else Judaism and Christianity contained, they both had a propensity to speculate. Greek philosophy, through its use of ideas and precise, flexible language, provides the means whereby profound reflection based upon intellection could take place.

The issues raised by the Wisdom literature of the Old Testament as well as the questions raised later by Greek Christians could now be dealt with. We must consider the merger of Judaeo-Christian religions and Greco-Roman thought in order to understand cultural, religious and institutional development in the West.

The answer to Tertullian's question: "What has Athens to do with Jerusalem?" is obvious. A great deal! The relation between faith and reason has been a preoccupation throughout Christian history, regardless of whether a believer is for or against reason. The reality of the encounter between Greek philosophy and the religions of revelation makes it so. The reality is: one must decide for or against *reason*. Usually one either uses reason to interpret what one believes, or one uses reason to argue why one renounces reason in the interpretation of what one believes. Ultimately, then, the choice has to do with the manner in which one chooses to use reason. One has only to recall the profound and subtle uses of philosophy in Karl Barth to observe this assumption.

Since our main interest is the way philosophy is used in *Christian* theology, I shall use only one example from Judaism, Philo. Philo initiated a tradition in philosophy which had an influence on the West for hundreds of years to come. He believed in the priority of revelation and subordinated philosophy to religious truth.

The Hellenization of Judaism

Philo was born in Alexandria about 20 B.C. His father was a man of influence and wealth in the Jewish congregation. Philo received the advantage of a good education and in his youth studied Greek philosophy. His writing was ornate in style, indicating a thorough knowledge of rhetoric. He was attracted to contemplation and philosophic wisdom for most of his life. Unlike his brother, who was a high official in the Roman administration of Egypt, Philo preferred a quiet life without worldly success or honors.

His life was interrupted by the policies of the Emperor Caligula, who required all Egyptians to worship him as a god. Since Jews were monotheists, Caligula developed a passionate hatred for them. In A.D. 38 Jews were subject to pogroms—they were attacked by angry mobs. The bloodshed to follow anticipated what we were to observe in the Nazi Holocaust. Philo was sent as a representative to Rome to negotiate in the midst of the crisis. The Jewish cause was aided by the assassination of Caligula. Peace was restored in Alexandria as well as in Palestine. Philo interpreted this peaceful resolution as God's providence. He felt that God's justice was vindicated.

Philo was a person with profound philosophical ability. But in spite of his training in Greek and Latin philosophy, he maintained his respect for religion. His guide was Moses rather than Aristotle; his inspiration was more from Jerusalem than from Athens.

Philo classifies humans in three ways: There are the "earth-born", the "heaven-born", and the "god-born." The earth-born are those who place priority upon the pleasures of the body. The heaven-born are attracted to art and learning. The god-born are priests and prophets who lived above mere sense-perceptions and who embrace the imperishable realities. According to Philo, the highest form of knowledge is not reason, but prophecy. And yet he has much appreciation for reason, which obtains a view of the essence of life.

But, the human mind is never independent of God. We cannot explain the human mind apart from the divine providence.

Self-knowledge is important, but it is not an end in itself. The more we know our innermost being, the more we realize our inadequacy. Reason can only develop by understanding its own inadequacy. When the divine Spirit enters the human soul, reason is evicted by being transcended. Mysticism demands emancipation from the senses. The last stage of knowledge, according to Philo, is a sense of fullness—we are recipients of divine grace. This stage is like a bright vision in which one views all things in their unity. This highest form of knowledge is given to the prophet rather than the philosopher. The prophet is the interpreter of God. We obtain this highest form of knowledge as a spiritual emancipation.

According to Philo, when compared with the Greeks, the Hebrews had the most adequate vision of God. Socrates was aware of the divine qualities in the universe, but his vision was inferior to Moses. It was the function of the Hebrew people to extend the message to God, to glorify his powers and extol his miracles. The function of the Greek mind, by contrast, was merely to systematize knowledge and to explain the universe in a rational manner. The Hebrews, according to Philo, were the people through whom humankind would be redeemed. They should, therefore, look beyond the oppression of the moment to a glorious future.

God exists as a unity. Philo's philosophy was theocentric in a monotheistic sense. God's providence is real and dependable. God is all-powerful and is not limited by material considerations. Like Plato, Philo explains the world by immaterial principles.

Teleology is at the center of Philo's philosophy. The lower parts of the universe are explained according to higher purposes. The realm of nature is subordinated to the realm of grace. Humans are inferior to angels, while angels are beneath God.

It is, however, impossible to know the divine essence because it is beyond reason. And yet the search for God is a worthy pursuit. Though the clear vision of God is denied us, we ought not to relinquish the quest. Being a mystic, Philo felt that a vision of God is possible. The category of reason can lead us to a reasonable probability, but this must be substantiated and superseded by the experiences of the prophets and the saints.

There is a special emphasis in Philo on the transcendence of God. The Greeks invested the gods with human qualities and their divine beings were infinite. In Philo the distance between God and humans are widened. Stress is laid upon the majesty of God and the nothingness of the human. And yet Philo did not despair of the human. The human remains dignified and important. God's transcendence does not mean that he is inert. God is beyond all reason, scientific laws or moral qualities, but God is not like Aristotle's unmoved mover. God is always active, creative and providentially engaged in the affairs in the world.

When asked how God rules the world or how his transcendence is combined with a material universe, Philo presents his *logos* doctrine. He is influenced by Heraclitus and the Stoics, but his metaphysical insights are distinctive. According to Philo, the *logos* is to be understood in various ways: 1. as God's essence: 2. as incorporeal being: and 3. as immanent wisdom. The *logos* exists as an immaterial essence in the mind of God, as a blueprint for the universe, and as an immanent quality in the world.

Philo's cosmic scheme demanded intermediaries. Angels were viewed as ambassadors between humans and God. He narrowly escapes polytheism here and seems to anticipate the medieval view. The latter position held that the universe was ruled not merely by God but by angels and saints, who assist in the salvation of humans.

The universe is created by God. It is not eternal as Aristotle had said. Philo rejected the plurality of worlds. This is the only universe, he declared. It is, however, indestructible and cannot be erased by a world conflagration.

Miracles are possible. All of creation testifies to the immense powers of God. Nature speaks with the voice of God. God uses supernatural phenomena to accomplish his purposes. Philo recalls what he believes to have been God's hand in Israel's history to support his view. It was through supernatural phenomena that God brought the Hebrews out of Egypt and sustained them through the long trek in the desert. Miracles, according to Philo, are a vital proof of the providence of God.

Wisdom is the goal of the fulfilled life. When one is serene and tranquil in mind as well as cheerful in actions, then one is in tune with God. Prayer and obedience to laws lead one in the direction of true piety. True knowledge is never opposed to religion or God. The more we study the divine books, the more we understand religion and the ways God works out his purposes in the universe. The ultimate aim of life is contemplation and mystical union. But we are to perfect ourselves in ordinary virtues. We must serve humans before we serve God.

It is asserted that contemplation can be found in two ways: alone in the wilderness, and through solitude even in society. The matter of primary importance is to cultivate a close relationship with God.

Philo appreciated asceticism. He admired the life and work of the Essenes. Again, he anticipates the medieval ideal of sainthood. His ethic went beyond Aristotle's secular existence based upon the Golden Mean and a rational appreciation of life. And, yet escapism is not the controlling principle of his philosophy. There is still hope in the future and one is expected to fulfill the duties of the practical life.

Philo's achievement is remarkable. He initiated a method in philosophy, in the West, based upon faith and revelation rather than systematized reason.

Philo's synthesis of religious and secular thinking is important for medieval thought. Humanism is replaced by a theocentric outlook. God becomes the standard for all of human actions, thoughts and ideals. Philo's *logos* doctrine is embraced by Christian theology. It showed how a mediation could be possible between a transcendent God and humans who live in two worlds, one material, the other spiritual.

Religion is expressed in concrete and tangible ways. Religion, according to Philo, is based on laws and revealed through prophecy. This is the expression of knowledge at its highest and best. Miracles are affirmed as those events which strengthen faith and reveal God's constant providence.

We meet a universalism in Philo based upon Mosaic laws rather than the Stoic system of ethics. According to Philo, the state is theocracy, not a moral commonwealth. Philo's ethic is more than a Hebraic version of Stoicism. Unlike the Stoics who embraced a materialistic atomism, Philo believed in the immaterial structure of the universe. And for him, the goal of life is more than apathy and tranquillity—it is the mystic vision through which humans understand the unity of the universe and achieve oneness with God.

I quote from conclusions I reached elsewhere:

There was stream of speculation which had begun to exercise a considerable influence upon the general current of men's thought at this point in history. The Alexandrian Jews entered readily into the intellectual life of Alexandria. They welcomed Greek philosophy as a further revelation in light of which the records of the Old Testament received a deeper meaning. In particular, the personifications of the Word and Wisdom of God, which had been described with gradually increasing clarity by the writers of some of the later books of the Old Testament, now found a counterpart in the conceptions of Plato and the other Greek philosophers. Jewish writers added to the purely ethical monotheism of their religion these new ideas, and this gave rise to the Jewish-Alexandrian School, of which Philo was the most distinguished representative.[1]

We shall return to Alexandria later to briefly look at Clement and Origen. But at this time, we will consider some of the earlier encounters between Christian theology and Greek philosophy. I am aware that from the beginnings of the Christian movement there has been a serious issue to be decided between faith and philosophy. In this chapter I shall attempt a summary of this developing relationship up to the time of Augustine. My selection is representative but not comprehensive. It should, however, indicate the logical connection between these two ways of knowing—faith and reason. The Gnostics, Marcion, some Apostolic Fathers, Clement and Origen will chart our course. We will then be prepared to examine the Augustinian synthesis which has influenced the remainder of Christian theological history.

Gnosticism[2]

Gnosticism was both Christian and non-Christian. The main thrust of Gnosticism was escape from this present evil world to the enjoyment of the blessings of a higher world of the spirit. The Gnostics were dualists who emphasized the contrast between spirit and matter. They set over against the material world in which humans live the invisible world of the spirit. How to obtain this higher world was their great concern. Like adherents to the mystical cults, the Gnostics sought salvation in mystical ways.

But Gnosticism was more than a mystery religion, it was also a philosophy. The Gnostics were interested in theology, cosmology and epistemology, which embraced all existence. There was no divorce between their philosophy and religion. For them, all philosophy was religiously motivated. Gnosticism was greatly influenced by Neo-Platonism. As philosophers the Gnostics were Neo-Platonists, but in essence they were religious devotees.

The Gnostics found in Christianity a program of salvation. It was therefore easy for them to accept much in Christian teachings. Since they were eclectic, they found it feasible to borrow profusely from ideas and practices of Christians. To those with a desire to obtain the higher world, Christianity had great appeal.

Christianity, especially as interpreted by Paul, was in some respects closely akin to their way of looking at things. A divine saviour through union with whom one may escape the flesh and enter a new spiritual life was very attractive. John's emphasis on knowledge was useful. Also, the understanding of the eucharist as feeding upon Christ had its appeal. They were not only attracted to Christianity, but joined the Christian movement in increasing numbers.

The Christian Gnostics transformed Christianity into a Gnostic religion of redemption. Most of the non-Christian Gnostics have been forgotten. The Christian Gnostics were people like Isidore of Alexandria and Valentinus of Rome. Unfortunately, most of their writings have also perished. We must rely, therefore, largely upon the anti-heretical writings for our knowledge of them. Most important are the reports of Irenaeus, Tertullian, Clement and Origen.

Dualism among the Gnostics was radical far beyond that of Platonism. There was obvious Zoroastrian influence. This was a dualism intensified and transformed into an absolute contradiction between matter and spirit, darkness and light—good and evil. One form of being was regarded as altogether excluding the other. Matter, according to the Gnostics, is not only independent of God and of a wholly different nature, but is radically and irredeemably evil. Gnostics were thorough-going pessimists with reference to the present life and order. Improvements were deemed impossible. The goal of salvation, therefore, was to escape from it all.

The kinship between the dualism of Paul and the Gnostics seems close. From an ethical point of view, Paul's dualism appears as extreme as the Gnostics. However, Paul's dualism lacked the ontological grounding which the Gnostics gave to their dualism. Paul had a doctrine of divine creation and providence which separated him from the Gnostics.

The Gnostics asserted that it was inconceivable that God could have created the evil in the world or could have had anything to do with it. Evil is explained by a series of divine emanations by which the nature of deity unfolds itself and is progressively depotentialized until it is adequately attenuated to endure contact with matter. The process of emanation was commonly represented in symbolic form as a process of generation. The successive emanations or aeons were personalized under the names of various qualities or attributes. These were arranged in pairs as male and female powers. This provided a dramatic and mythical character for their cosmology.

The Christian Fathers who criticized the Gnostics for their heresy pointed to the similarity of the activity of the aeons to the love affairs of heathen gods. They saw this as a revival of Greek polytheism and were not open to an in-depth understanding of the Gnostics. The Gnostics themselves, however, had a different understanding. The aeons were meant only as a symbolic rendering of the great process of evolution or devolution by which the world had come to be.

The existence of the world was explained by the activity of one of the lowest in the series of aeons, far removed from the supreme God—the source of all divinity. This lowly aeon was either ignorant of the supreme God or hostile toward him. Thus working alone or in cooperation with angels, this single aeon bridged the gap between the realms of spirit and matter. This activity brought order out of chaos. The aeon became the world-creator, or demiurge, as he was generally called. Into the world thus formed sparks of divinity were introduced. Tradition has it that these sparks of divinity were introduced not by the demiurge himself, but by a higher and more spiritual aeon without his knowledge.

These sparks of divinity found a lodgment in humans, and those who were thus endowed lived henceforth in an alien world far from their true home. They longed to be released and restored to the divine realm where they belonged. This hunger for release from bondage in an alien world became the great religious problem for the Gnostics. Salvation meant a radical break with the past. It meant an escape from the world to be with God—release from the flesh to live the life of the spirit. The flesh was believed to be necessarily and unalterably evil.

Paul was seized upon as an ally. He seemed to be in basic agreement with the Gnostics as he viewed the human condition. Paul insisted that it is impossible for humans to attain salvation by themselves—God must save them. The Gnostics were quick to seize on that part of the gospel as their answer. The Christ whom Paul proclaimed was just the savior they thought they needed. The Gnostics did not understand Christ to be a Messiah who came to establish the reign of God on earth. For them, Christ was not the founder of a religious crusade. Rather, Christ was a divine being by mystical union, with whom they might become partakers of the divine nature and return to the higher realm. Thus, it was the Christ-mysticism in Paul that claimed their attention and met their needs.

Even before the time of Christ, however, Gnostics had a myth of a divine savior. It was, therefore, natural for them to combine this figure with Christ. They identified Christ with one of the highest aeons and taught that he came down from above to rescue the spirits of humans. But in their view he did not become man, was not born of woman, and did not suffer and die.

According to the Gnostics, all humans are not in line for salvation. A type of election or predestination is apparent in their system. The masses have animal souls and will perish. Only those who possess a spark of the divine or a spiritual nature implanted from above can be saved.

The role of the savior was to reveal to the elect the way of life they should live. His task was to free them from the control of demons, to liberate them from the prison (of the body) and restore them to the higher world.

"*Gnosis*" or knowledge is the principal means of salvation. One of their favorite verses was John 17:3: "This is life eternal, *to know* the only true God and Jesus Christ who thou hast sent." *Gnosis*, however, had primarily a religious rather than a philosophical connotation. *Gnosis* was a synonym for the pneumatic or spiritual. It refers not merely to intellectual apprehension of truth as the result of observation or reflection, but indicates an immediate vision of the divine, particularly of God. *Gnosis* as used by the Gnostics took on a mystical character.

Knowledge was by revelation from God. It included knowledge of the world, of human life, and things, but it was first of all religious and saving knowledge. It might develop into philosophy, but its primary attribute was a vision of God and oneness with him. This saving knowledge of God might be mediated by rites, ceremonies and sacraments. Mysteries had a place in this system if they facilitated union with God and purified the soul from sin. Knowledge, from whatever source, was intended to impart power to overcome evil and to enhance the higher life. The goal of salvation was the journey of the soul to the highest realm of the spirit.

Salvation could be prompted by good conduct as well. For example, the flesh must be subdued and seduced by asceticism. Some Gnostics took the opposite position of libertinism: that is, giving free rein to the passions. Students of world religions are familiar with such responses to a preoccupation with overcoming evil. For example, in Hinduism, tanticism exists side by side with the most rigorous forms of asceticism—to the same end of salvation or liberation.

Gnosticism was generally hostile to Judaism. The reason appears to be that Judaism affirms the goodness of creation. Apparently, the Gnostics overlooked the carry-over of this belief into Christianity. Or, conversely, they saw in Christianity other things they liked and seized upon these. For the Gnostics, God is a saving God—not a creating God. Salvation is the opposite of creation and represents its denial and defeat. The world was created by the demiurge—not by the supreme God. The Old Testament, if recognized at all, was ascribed to the demiurge rather than to the supreme God.

I believe this interaction between Gnostics and Christians to be important. It illustrates a crucial encounter between Christianity and a non-Christian religious philosophy which developed in the same historical and cultural milieu as formative Christianity. This challenge and the Christian response illustrate the need for Christians sometimes to be prepared to support their faith through rigorous intellectual reflection.

The Christian Apologists

The Christian Apologists shared with the Gnostics the desire to make the Christian religion more intelligible.[3] They appealed to philosophy in their defense against non-believers as well as in response to the Gnostics. They viewed Christianity as both a philosophy and a revelation. The truths of Christianity were of supernatural origin and absolutely certain, but they were also rational—even if they could be fully comprehended by a divinely inspired mind.

Like Schleiermacher, the Apologists directed their thought toward the "cultured despisers" of the faith. They were acquainted with the literature and philosophy of their times and targeted the educated classes. Many of these church leaders were highly educated and cultured. They saw their mission as that of interpreting the Christian faith among the literate and educated. This is why the philosophical element predominates in their writings, and why the purely religious aspect is often relegated to the background. We will discuss here Justin, Irenaeus and Origen as representative of the views of the Apologists.[4]

Justin the Martyr

Justin the Martyr left two important works, the *Dialogue* and the *Apology*. The *Apology* was written shortly after 150. In it Justin undertook to define Christianity and commend it to the favorable attention of the rulers of the state. The *Dialogue* consists of conversations, perhaps imaginary, with a Jew called Trypho. It aims to show from Hebrew prophecy that Christianity has replaced Judaism in God's purpose. Jews, therefore, as well as Gentiles, can be saved only through Jesus Christ. Both works agree on essentials. The works were written to win new converts, but were also intended to strengthen the faith to those who were already Christians.[5]

Justin was by profession an able philosopher. He studied Stoicism, Aristotelianism and Pythagoreanism.[6]

It was the last-mentioned that most excited him. According to Justin, philosophy is honorable before God. God leads and unites us in the use of the mind as a sacred deed. Philosophical knowledge can lead to truth and real happiness.

It was through an encounter with an aged Christian that Justin was converted to Christianity. His conversation account touches upon several subjects: philosophy, knowledge of God and immortality. The Christian provided a testimony and then left. But Justin was moved by powerful thoughts. He recalls: ". . . A fire was kindled in my soul and I was seized with love for the prophets and for the friends of Jesus."[7]

Justin immediately began to apply his philosophical interest to Christianity. What he really discovered was an assurance for the highest and best thought he knew. Since his interest was practical, he was greatly impressed by the moral philosophy present around him.

According to Justin, the essence of philosophy is the knowledge of God. Plato taught that God can be known by natural reason, for God and humans share a kinship. Justin formerly agreed with this Platonic notion. But through his understanding of Christian faith he now held a different view. God can be known only by revelation. Humans can know many things by reason alone, but such knowledge is abstract. It lacks the clarity and particularity which the assurance of revelation brings.

God is a moral ruler who demands righteousness. He rewards the good and punishes the wicked. Humans have free will and may live righteous lives if they choose.[8] All virtue is independent—we determine our own character by the choices we make. Repentance initiates the Christian life. It is rewarded by divine forgiveness. Repentance and forgiveness are to be followed by a life of virtue and obedience to the law of God. Virtues are viewed as kindness and purity. Love is strongly emphasized. Justin advocates love for all, including enemies. He did not choose asceticism, but had high praise for those who lived a celibate life. He saw love for God and neighbor as the law of God which replaces the legalism of the Jews.

Justin found it easy to explain the Messiahship of Jesus. But the divinity of Christ drove him to reconsider *logos* philosophy.

For Justin, *logos* means both *reason* and *word*. He was perhaps inspired by the prologue to the Gospel of John, but he used the term *logos* for a decidedly apologetic purpose. The Stoics had used the term to designate divine forces resident in the world. The Platonists had used it to describe intermediate beings or agents which bridged the chasm between God and the universe, and made it possible for God to communicate with the world and act upon it. Justin wanted to emphasize the philosophical character of Christianity and commend it to profound thinkers. But he wanted most of all to enhance the authority and significance of Christ.

The Logos is the divine reason, begotten before the creation of the world and employed by God as his agent in creation. He is a personal being, identical with the second God of the Old Testament theophanies and also with Christ, in whom he has become incarnate. And, yes, Justin often uses the word *logos* in an original philosophical sense to mean human or divine reason.

All knowledge and truth is owed to the divine Logos—whether truth is direct or indirect. The Logos spoke through the prophets and is incarnate in Jesus Christ. Christ had the whole Logos (body, soul, mind). As a consequence, all who possess truth possess Christ and are recognized as Christians. This includes Socrates and other philosophers as well as patriarchs and prophets. Every race of humans partakes of the Logos. All who lived rationally are Christians, even if they are believed to be atheists. Justin was not just attempting to be broadminded; he mainly desired to emphasize the universal influence and authority of Christ.

Justin insists that the truth discovered by Moses was more ancient than that of the Greeks. The Greeks acquired whatever truth they have from the Logos to whom Moses and the prophets owed the truth they knew. In sum, Justin stressed the essence of Christianity and its agreement and confirmation of the best philosophical, moral and religious thought he knew. In this manner, faith and reason were brought together.

Irenaeus

Irenaeus, bishop of Lyons in Gaul in the late second century, was a creative and original thinker. He was an influential theologian of the early church, and combined the legal and mystical elements of the theology of his day. Born in Asia Minor, he later lived in Gaul and visited Rome frequently; he was an admirer of Justin and was against the Gnostics. In fact, it was his response to Gnosticism which informed his formulation of the meaning of Christianity as he understood it. His two most important works are *Against Heresy* (five books) and *Demonstration of Apostolic Preaching*. The former is most important in understanding his theology, but it is unsystematic, being mainly devoted to anti-Gnostic polemics. Irenaeus's writings were produced in Greek, but survived in Latin—where one cannot always be sure of the translation. Fortunately, important fragments exist in Greek. This makes it possible to spot-check the accuracy of some important passages.

The nature of salvation was of great importance to Irenaeus. Salvation has two stages, one negative, the other positive. The negative aspect has to do with release from the power of Satan. The latter points to the attainment of immortality. Salvation is not complete until one experiences release from sin and immortality. Salvation is necessary because of Adam's fall. The Fall had two effects: it brought humans under the control of Satan, and deprived us of our likeness to God or the immortality with which we were originally endowed. Salvation is release from the control of Satan and reclaiming one's immortality.

Release from Satan is made possible by the work of Christ—a work of perfect obedience. Christ ascended, while Adam descended. The Logos recapitulates Adam himself, and is viewed as the counterpart of Adam. In this spirit, Irenaeus views the Decalogue as a summary of natural law and as binding upon Christians.

According to Irenaeus, the substance of life is *participation* in God. A vision of God is the means by which we enter into immortal life.[9] He so emphasizes participation in God as to suggest deification. Salvation involves the transformation of human nature into the divine, the mortal into the immortal, immortality being the distinguishing characteristic of deity.[10] Irenaeus shared this concept of deification with the mystery religions, the Stoics, the Cynics and the

Platonists. For him, this experience of deification was the very heart of Christianity.[11]

If Irenaeus's view of immortality is Greek, his understanding of the resurrection appears to be otherwise. Salvation, according to Irenaeus, includes the flesh as well as the spirit. Thus he believed in the resurrection of the flesh.[12] In this belief he was consistent with most first- and second-century Christians except Paul and the Gnostics. The Gnostics were completely anti-body in their view of the afterlife. Paul reflects rabbinic as well as Hellenistic influences in his view of the resurrection (I Cor. 15).

In his christology, Irenaeus is consistent with his general understanding of salvation. Christ won a victory over sin and over Satan. But beyond this, his doctrine of incarnation illustrates a creative mind at work. According to Irenaeus, the incarnation is based upon the union of the divine and human natures in Christ. In this process the human nature, in Christ, was deified, giving it the quality of immortal life. Irenaeus states his case: "The Logos of God, our Lord Jesus Christ, who on account of his great love became what we are that he might make us what he is in himself."[13]

Humans cannot be changed into the divine status unless God is changed into a human status. The Logos of God assumed humanity, and the one who was the Son of God became the son of humans, that this one, having contained the Logos and having received the adoption, might become the Son of God. In other words, the goal of salvation is deification. But we cannot receive immortality. This cannot take place unless first incorruptibility and immortality have been made what we are. Thereafter, the corruptible may be absorbed by incorruptibility and the mortal by immortality and we receive the adoption of sons/daughters.[14]

Christ had to be God to save us. If he had been merely a subordinate divinity or a being of a different nature from God, incarnation would not be complete. His incarnation would not have united God and humanity and, therefore, humans would have remained mortal and unsaved. Irenaeus conceived of the incarnation of the Logos in his own way. He refused to subordinate the Logos to God as some other Apologists did. Irenaeus insists upon a two-fold generation of the Son, from the Father and from the Virgin. Son of God is used in the double sense of pre-existent Logos and the historic figure of Jesus Christ.[15]

Irenaeus goes on to identify God and the Logos, or Son, completely. The Logos is God in the fullest sense, but he is God revealed, not God apart from the world and creatures. The Father is the invisible of the Son and the Son is the visible of the Father. God is all mind and Logos.[16] What he thinks he says and what he says he is thinking. His thought is Logos and Logos is mind. The Mind which comprehends all things is itself the Father.[17]

It is significant that Irenaeus argues vigorously for the humanity of Christ. He goes so far as to say that Christ lived to be fifty. This made it possible for him to identify with the various stages of human life: infancy, childhood, youth, middle life, etc. The death and resurrection of the earthly Jesus seem to have no importance. Divine life is bestowed by the union of God and the human brought about in the Incarnation. Flesh and spirit share in the experience of salvation.

Salvation is by obedience and through the knowledge of God. Baptism and eucharist are means of salvation. Thus, Irenaeus develops a sacramental theology and lays a foundation for the Catholic system. He brings the ethico-legal and the mystical strands of theology together. In some ways, he saved the Old Testament for the church. He showed Christians why they should retain the moral law of the Jews while rejecting the ceremonial laws. His view of revelation was progressive and culminated in the Incarnation. Irenaeus interpreted the work of Christ in such a manner as to give saving value to all aspects of the life of Christ. He provided a foundation for belief in the resurrection of the flesh. He placed the sacraments of baptism and eucharist at the heart of Christianity. He re-read and reclaimed Paul who had been rendered suspect by Gnostic interpretation. It is the revised interpretation of Paul by Irenaeus that has survived most in Christian theological history.

Origen

Our final discussion, before we consider Augustine, is of two great thinkers, again in Alexandria. Clement and Origen were Neo-Platonic thinkers. They were Christian, but in the tradition of Philo. Platonism appears in full force in the Catechical School of Alexandria. Clement (died 216) was the first head of this school; he was followed by Origen (175–254). Origen brought Christianity and philosophy together in the third century. The work of Plotinus had a direct influence upon him.

Origen's project was to assimilate the classical philosophy of immaterialism with Christianity. He succeeded in providing the framers of the Nicene Creed with a formula they could use. However, his remarkable achievement had an intrinsic problem. It was imbedded in a powerful neo-Platonic framework which was antithetical to the revelational point of view of Athanasius. In a few words, the philosophical spirit of Origen was in conflict with the faith position espoused by Athanasius, bishop of Alexandria, and architect of later christology. It was Athanasius who won out. And, yet, in Origen the encounter between philosophy and Christianity reached a superb moment of profound reflection, which deserves careful attention. I attempt to encapsulate his profound insights briefly here.

In Origen's treatise *On First Principles* (of Christian philosophy) we encounter a culmination of the movement in Alexandria initiated by Philo. Plotinus was a contemporary of Origen. Some Gnostics were in the same tradition. The contemporary influences provide a context for understanding Origen.

Origen's God is transcendent in the extreme sense affirmed by Plotinus. He is absolute and a simple unity, beyond thought and being. In accounting for the universe of change and matter, Origen makes full use of the Neo-Platonic explanation. There is an emanation from the transcendent and immaterial principle through an intermediary. This subordinated role, of intermediary, is assigned to Christ. Christ is conceived of as the Logos or as the hypostatized Divine Wisdom of the transcendent deity. That is to say, Christ is of the same essence as God, distinct but not separate, like the sunbeam to the sun. Christ is generated, eternally. There never was a time when the sun did not exist. However, Origen insists upon a distinction between Father and Son. Although the Son is generated of the essence of the Father, he is an eternally distinct divine *hypostasis*.

The Son is not in the world of change, but is close to it as a go-between. He contains the pattern or archetype of the multiplicity of existences of the world of spirit. Of these rational existences, timelessly created by the Son or Logos, the Holy Spirit is inferior to the Son, as the Son is inferior to the Father. All other rational existences are less in status than the Holy Spirit. Among the lesser rational existences are immaterial souls which are equal in the possession of freedom (free will). But by the exercise of this freedom, some have become deficient in love, have declined from their original state, and are imprisoned in the world of matter; thus they have developed in a manner contrary to their original purpose. These fallen existences may rise from this low estate and ascend to their original spiritual state through a belief in Christ, a pure spirit. If Origen's confession about faith in Christ is based upon the Christian revelation, his thought-orientation is clearly neo-Platonic. In a real sense his christology seems to be lost in neo-Platonic philosophy.

It is not difficult to understand why this position was attacked in the third century by Christian theologians who were not under the spell of Neo-Platonism. In the fourth century there was a full-scale classical reaction against Origen's position. Augustine, for example, does not get his incentive from Origen, but from the doctrine of the church expressed through the creeds and not through speculation alone. The Council of Nicea used Origen's formula as a structure to oppose Arius, whose thought was in basic agreement with Origen. The Council turned to scripture rather than to philosophy to justify the hypostatic union of the divine and human in Christ. We are therefore able to observe at Nicea a change in the relation of theology to philosophy from what one sees in Origen as well as others akin to him. The church forges its creeds out of its own tradition and then takes philosophy into its service. The theologians of the church cut the umbilical cord of its dependence upon the Greek philosophical tradition. The church launched its own intellectual tradition, anchored in its own thought-developments. But philosophy is enlisted in the service of theology.

Athanasius

Athanasius, bishop of Alexandria (c. 296–373) represents the new outlook which indicates an important state of maturation for Christian theology. Under him, the church insisted that although one could distinguish the divine that was incarnate in Jesus from other aspects of deity, it was co-equal with those other aspects and participated equally with them in deity itself. Deity itself was incarnate in Jesus. There is only one deity which by its very nature is both immanent and transcendent. In Athanasius, theology takes its own high ground. It is not so much the content of Athanasius' thought as his outlook which provides a foundation for the remarkable place of Augustine in Christian intellectual history.

VI

Augustine and the Primacy of Faith in the Middle Ages

Augustine: The Man

Augustine was born in Tagaste, North Africa, in 353 or 354, of a non-Christian father and a Christian mother, Monica. His mother exercised a profound influence upon her son. He became a teacher of rhetoric, first in his native city, later in Milan (384–6). His preoccupation with philosophical and religious questions led him from Manichaeism to Skepticism, and yet he was unsatisfied. In 386 he began to read Plato and Plotinus. Through these philosophers he gained stability of thought. It was about this same time that he came under the influence of Ambrose, Bishop of Milan. After his conversion in 387, Augustine returned to Tagaste. There he remained for three years, lived according to monastic rules, and was ordained to the priesthood. In 396 he was raised to the bishopric of Hippo, in Africa, where he served until his death in 430. He wrote many important works. Among these are: *Freedom of Will, The True Religion, Predestination and Grace, The Trinity, The City of God, Confessions* and *Letters*. Fortunately, his writings are available and have met the test of time.[1]

Early Thought

Manichaeism

Augustine tells us that in his nineteenth year he was inflamed with an ardent desire for wisdom through reading Cicero's *Hortensius*.[2]

He discovered Manichaeism, which combined a Persian dualistic cosmology of light and darkness with a religious belief in ascetic discipline aimed at setting the soul free from the forces of darkness. In this sect, good was associated with light, evil with darkness, just as the world of reason or *logos* was identified with fire by the Stoics. Manichaeism seems to have appealed to Augustine for several reasons: its notion of God as refined material substance, light; its explanation of natural and moral evil as the result of a cosmic principle of darkness; its offer of redemption from bondage or darkness and evil; the fact that Christ, whom he had learned from his mother, was a prophet; and the Manichaean claim that their teachings would be accepted by reason rather than by authority alone.

Neo-Platonism

Neo-Platonism provided Augustine with answers to his philosophical questions as well as with a worthy object of religious devotion.[3] Augustine tells us that the Platonists enabled him to conceive God in spiritual rather than material terms. They offered him a cosmology in which the Good is the ultimate ground of all things in the visible world. They asserted that evil has no substantial reality, but is only a privation or defect of that which is good.[4] They awakened in him the spiritual desire to lift himself above the inferior and transitory things of time to mystical union with God, the eternal and unchangeable Light of Truth.[5]

Augustine was to learn, however, that there were limitations to neo-Platonism. Neo-Platonism points us to the end of the soul's journey: union with God as well as the unchanging and perfect Good. It cannot, however, show us the *way* to that goal.[6] The soul might on rare occasions catch a glimpse of the Good and be filled with joy—but it could not sustain itself on those heights of the spirit when images from the sensible world crowded into it and drew its attention back to corporeal things.[7] Augustine had embraced Neo-Platonism, intellectually, but his will remained unconvinced. He found himself wavering between devotion to the eternal God, at one time, but, at another time, being pulled downward to lust and pride.

The will had to be radically changed and brought into unity with itself before it could really love God and obtain peace and joy. This is what Augustine's conversion in Milan, precipitated by the reading of a passage from Paul (Rom. 13:13-14), accomplished. As he read "put on the Lord Jesus Christ," the disquiet of his conflicting desires was dissolved and his besetting sins of sensuality and pride began to fall away.[8] While Neo-Platonism provided the intellectual bridge over which Augustine passed from Manichaeism and Skepticism to Christianity, he came to see a difference between Neo-Platonism and the God of Christianity and the human relation to this God.

Let us be more specific! Augustine read in the Platonists that "the Word was God." This would appear to be the Mind or *Nous* of Plotinus. But what was not there was that "the Word was made flesh and dwelt amongst us," and that "in due time Christ died for the ungodly." The Christian belief in the Incarnation implied a conception of God different from Neo-Platonism.[9] The God of Christians was not the impersonal transcendent "One" of Plotinus, but the personal God of the Bible who had stooped to man's need by manifesting his love in Christ.

Humans, according to Augustine's understanding, cannot elevate themselves by moral and intellectual effort to mystical union with God. They cannot attain salvation themselves. This is because the human will is in bondage to itself. Self-love obstructs the human will from proper devotion to God. Only God's love can awaken the human will so that it yearns for the love of God, which is the only means to salvation. Augustine's conversion to Christianity not only transformed his heart and will, but it led him to rethink many of his prior intellectual conclusions.

Étienne Gilson makes important observations on the above point. He asserts that Augustine owed almost all the matter and technique of his philosophy to Plotinus, but that he drew from the Bible such basic Christian beliefs as those which compelled him to make inner changes which separated him from the Plotinian program of salvation. Augustine, therefore, constructed a different and original thought-system to undergird his experience of salvation. It is Gilson's conclusion that Augustine was very successful in that effort. He went on to develop a philosophical theology which is the first and best and most original contribution to Christian thought.[10]

Another way of stating the case is to say that Augustine's metaphysical and epistemological concepts are fundamentally Neo-Platonic. His understanding of God, humanity, history and other doctrines of the Christian faith are very different. It is among the latter conceptions that Augustine's intellectual genius is manifest in its most creative and original form of expression. The Neo-Platonic influences upon him were profound in strictly philosophical matters. However, he made radical modifications to them in his interpretation of Christian beliefs. So his contribution to Christianity is not superficial, but profound. Ever since his time we have had to reckon with that contribution. We need to remember, however, that Augustine was also human. His contribution is limited by this fact, and by a heavy reliance on his personal experience of salvation. Our examination of his thought will be appreciative but critical.

Faith Seeking Understanding

Knowledge and illumination are key conceptions in Augustine's thought. He has a practical and existential understanding of philosophy. In his thought "wisdom" is always related to "happiness." Augustine wishes to find the kind of good, the possession of which will satisfy desire and ensure peace. This *eudaemonism* (well-being) can be explained by the fact that he always regarded philosophy as something quite different from the speculative pursuit of the knowledge of nature. He was concerned most of all with the problem of his own destiny. For Augustine, the important thing was to strive for self-knowledge and to learn the means to greater happiness. Happiness is not understood in a hedonistic sense with reference to physical pleasure. It is understood, rather, in a qualitative sense akin to blessedness.

Augustine is mainly concerned with human life. The knowledge of truth is essential to happiness. Blessedness requires the attainment of the knowledge of the good as well. The purpose of philosophy is to seek "wisdom," *sapientia*, concerning the Good, which is both permanent and independent of the changes in philosophy. The proper function of philosophy is to seek knowledge, not primarily for its own sake, but for the sake of the Good. One must not merely contemplate the Good, but enjoy and love it.

Philosophy must identify with the truth and possess it, if it is to obtain true knowledge. This is an important reason why Skepticism did not satisfy Augustine. It was necessary for him to have a positive theory of knowledge. He could not live with a theory of "probability" as far as knowledge is concerned.[11] He asserts that we cannot know that a proposition is "like" the truth unless we know the truth. We may make mistakes in interpreting sense impressions, but sense impressions as such never deceive us and are always true. The fact that an oar appears bent in the water does not mean that it is really so. In fact, if the law of refraction is not to be violated, it must appear bent. Again we have certain knowledge of mathematical and ethical truths.[12]

Augustine seems to anticipate Descartes' *"cogito, ergo sum,"* "I think, therefore I am." But Augustine was not concerned about the existence of the external worlds in the sense that Descartes was. Augustine knew that the senses add much to natural knowledge. According to Augustine, corporeal objects are the proper objects of the intellect, but they are merely the starting point of the ascent of the mind to God. He had little interest in the natural world. He was seeking for truth as a necessary condition of the blessedness of the soul. His main intellectual interest was with two things: God and the soul.

When we consider Augustine's view of rational knowledge, the impact of Platonism is very evident. Although the objects of true knowledge must be unchanging, humans can have rational knowledge of corporeal things by judging them according to eternal Ideas or standards. When he judges that one thing excels another in beauty, he does so according to an eternal standard of beauty. When he asserts that a line is straight or that a circle is well drawn, he implies a reference to the Idea of straightness or circularity. Rational knowledge is called *scientia* over against *sapientia* or wisdom. Since rational knowledge requires an appeal to the senses, it is intermediate between sense knowledge and wisdom.

Wisdom arises when the mind turns away from the things of the senses to contemplate eternal and immutable Truth. At first sight, it may appear to be nothing more than a certain kind of science, since it, too, is rational and possesses absolute certainty. However, it must be distinguished from science, which concentrates upon changeable things and tempts the mind to neglect unchangeable Truth. If, however, the mind were left to its own inclinations, it would devote its attention mainly to knowing intelligibles—because the mind is at home in the exercise of pure contemplation, without thought of action.

In the present life, however, the soul has as one of its main functions the governing of the body. In order to fulfill that function, the soul gets involved in action. Humans are compelled to make use of things and to do this we must know them. Hence the mind must be employed in purposes other than contemplation.[13]

Reason, according to Augustine, may be directed upward or downward. It is up to us to decide the direction it will move. The decision is very important. If one chooses the superior reason, one's thought will turn toward the divine Ideas, to Wisdom. On the other hand, if one selects "inferior" reason, one will turn to corporeal things in order to exploit and enjoy them for one's private ends. The choice is determined by the nature of one's will and the direction of one's character. It requires humility to submit oneself to the divine order and live as part of the whole. The alternative is to yield to pride and fall into covetousness. One therefore chooses to seek one's own satisfaction and exalts the part rather than the whole. One seeks to possess all for oneself and neglects others. In this way epistemology and ethics are interdependent.

The relation between wisdom and science requires more clarification. Wisdom alone can bring blessedness. It would therefore seem best to refuse science and choose wisdom. A closer look indicates that what Augustine proposes is not rejection, but the subordination of science. The soul regulates itself as well as temporal things in the service of the eternal—it must therefore know them. When science is used in this way as an instrument of wisdom, it is legitimate and necessary. We are often tempted to use it otherwise— out of pride and for selfish ends. Humans tend to have one character when they let wisdom reign and another when the lower appetites are in control. Only when we seek wisdom is there a proper balance between sense knowledge of material things and the pure intuition of divine Ideas.

Rational knowledge is made possible by the judgment of corporeal things in relation to eternal Ideas. Augustine accepted the Neo-Platonic view that the Ideas belong not to an impersonal realm of essences but to the divine Mind. Ideas are archetypal forms and immutable essences of things, which have not themselves been formed, but exist eternally and unchangeably in the divine intelligence.[14]

Illumination as a conception in Augustine's thought presents a challenge to any interpreter. There are at least two ways in which scholars have viewed this important conception. Some hold that since the contents of the divine mind must be identified with the divine essence, to see the Ideas in the divine Mind must involve an immediate intuition of the divine essence of God. Others insist that God actively infuses into our minds the Ideas by which we judge things and that our minds are passive with respect to them.

Augustine does not provide a clear account of how we are to understand divine illumination. There is, however, an obvious Platonic influence. He speaks, for example, of God who illumines the Ideas of the intelligible world in the manner in which the sun illuminates the objects of the sensible world. Again, he insists that mathematical Ideas cannot be known unless they are illuminated by something else corresponding to the sun and implies this light is God. At another time, he speaks of the Intelligible Light through whom all intelligible things are illuminated. The divine Light somehow makes the eternal Truths visible to the human mind. This illumination is made possible by the fact that God is the Truth in whom all things participate.[15]

According to Gilson, we glean a clearer understanding of what Augustine means by divine illumination. Divine illumination makes it possible for our intellect to see the truth of its own judgment and the necessity it implies. For instance, experience can account for the formation of the idea of a work of art, but necessity and certitude of judgment that it is beautiful cannot be explained by experience alone. Experience and not illumination tells us what the particular object is, while illumination tells us what the object in its perfect state ought to be. The action of the divine Ideas on the mind does not imply ontologism (being *qua* being) because action is essentially "regulative" and does not involve content. The divine idea is not knowledge which passes ready-made from the divine mind to the human mind. In "mystical" knowledge, the mind attains a vision of the divine Ideas and the divine light themselves. But in natural knowledge, the divine illumination only makes possible judgments of truth which are necessary and certain.[16]

Our faith seeks understanding. Natural knowledge can be attained by the use of the senses and reason without the aid of faith. But according to Augustine the supernatural knowledge which is necessary to salvation must be based upon faith. Belief is thought to be accompanied by assent.

Belief, far from being limited to the acceptance of revealed truth, is a natural and necessary act of thought which plays a large part in our life. Many opinions are beliefs which are based on the witness of others, and some of these beliefs are indispensable to our personal and social existence. For instance, one may believe that a certain man is one's father solely on the authority of one's mother. One may also believe that a particular woman is one's mother based on the authority of a nurse. One's family ties may well be based upon such beliefs.

We believe in past events we have not seen, based upon the reports of those who witness to us. Thus in the case of religious beliefs we put our trust in the reports of historical events. For example, witnesses report the life of Christ and the power he exerted upon their lives, and we base our faith in such reports. Of course, our acceptance of the authority of these Christian witnesses must be based upon evidence that they are trustworthy and that belief in Christ is true. Augustine depends for his evidence largely upon the remarkable impact and spread of Christianity in the first three centuries—its spread throughout the Mediterranean world by the time of his conversion.

According to Augustine, it is reasonable that reason should not refuse the assistance of faith in its task. One will not seek God diligently if one does not believe that God exists. He states his position in this often-quoted statement: "Therefore do not seek to understand in order to believe, but believe that thou mayst understand; since, 'Except ye believe, ye shall not understand.' "[17]

Why does Augustine hold that faith is prior to understanding? One reason is that reason is fallen. Reason is not in the state it was originally created. It has been distorted by sin. It cannot attain the wisdom whose object is God because it has been turned away by pride from eternal things to the changing things of the senses.

Furthermore, we who have deformed the image of God in ourselves cannot reform it; only God who made it can remake it. Reason, therefore, requires help from above to do, in it and for it, things it cannot do alone. Reason, far from despising itself, asks God for faith to purify the heart, so that by freeing itself from the stain of sin it may be able to increase its light and be whole again. In brief, the purification of the heart by faith is a necessary condition for the illumination of the mind. Faith must transform the heart before reason can be restored to health.[18]

Natural reason without the assistance of faith is able to attain rational knowledge. For instance, the knowledge of mathematical and ethical truths may be acquired without faith. Natural reason may even attain a kind of knowledge *about* God. Augustine recalled that the followers of Plato entertain such an idea of God as to admit that in him are to be found the cause of existence, the ultimate reason for the understanding, and the end in reference to which the whole world is to be regulated. But this knowledge is imperfect and ineffective because it does not involve acknowledgment by the will or lead to love. He goes on to point out that in spite of the knowledge of God among the Greek philosophers, they did not renounce polytheism.

All of this centers upon Augustine's assertion that the will has a powerful effect upon knowledge. What is known cannot be separated from what is loved. All cognition is directly dependent upon one's interest. Nothing is fully known to which the consent of the will has not been given. Yet there may be awareness of reality without completed cognition of that reality. The completion of cognition lies with affection. God may be known without being acknowledged. This is a description of Augustine's understanding of the human condition.

Augustine held that in the process of knowing, the cognitive faculty, *ratio*, takes in according to its power, reality both temporal and eternal. It is, however, primarily passive or neutral and its recognition is limited to that which is dominant in the mind. The will is the controlling factor. That which is known is precisely that which is passionately loved. Humans have fallen under the sway of sinful pride and have turned away from the love of God, *amor Dei*, to the love of self, *amor sui*. In making self rather than God the object of our dominant affection, we have perverted our reason. We have redirected reason from its true function of contemplating the eternal Ideas and God himself. The only remedy to this state of affairs is for our wills to be cleansed through submission to faith in Christ. We must follow his example of humility.

Augustine insists upon the priority of faith over against reason. A comparison with Aristotle will help clarify this point. Aristotle presents an intellectualism in which reason has the ascendancy. According to Aristotle, desire or will follows upon cognition. Ideal knowledge is the pure contemplation of Being without regard to practical concerns. Augustine, on the other hand, maintains that knowledge depends upon what one wills or loves. The intellectualist refuses commitment until reason has seen. But, according to Augustine, the reason cannot have sight until it yields to commitment. Since it is only the love of God which can supplant human perverse love of self and temporal things, faith must awaken love to bring about a renewal of our understanding.

Faith, however, is not the ultimate goal of our quest for divine truth. Understanding should follow faith. Thus his statement: "Unless you believe, you will not understand." So what Augustine has in mind is not an immature, blind faith, but a faith, culminating in understanding. This is the basis of his famous formula "*fides quaerens intellectum*," or "faith seeking understanding." To believe in God is not the end of humans; it is eternal life *to know* God. We begin in faith and we are made perfect by sight. Faith, then, is not its own end. It is merely the token of knowledge which is vaguely sketched out here below, but will be fully expanded in life eternal.

Augustine does not make a radical distinction between philosophical and theological truths because they are so closely related in his thought. All the truths that are essential for blessedness are revealed in scripture and must be believed. On the other hand, our reason can attain some understanding of everyone of them if it seeks to do so. All revealed truths can be known to some extent at least, but none of them can be exhausted, since they have God as their ultimate object. The difference between the various things to which our minds are applied is simply that some of them can be known clearly, others vaguely and still others hardly at all.

The existence of evil and the meaning of the Trinity are examples. According to Augustine, while we can understand how evil can exist in a world created by God, we cannot demonstrate or even make intelligible to ourselves the Trinity. And yet, Augustine insists that the mystery of the Trinity does not completely escape our understanding. We can find analogies for the Trinity in our mind, which is made in the image of God. It follows that Augustine does not attempt to establish, as Aquinas was to do, a line of demarcation between rational and revealed theology.

The development of other topics treated by Augustine such as creation and evil, the existence of God, the philosophy of history, the Trinity, etc., would further illustrate his epistemology. We, however, are mainly concerned about his theory of knowledge. We have attempted to state and illustrate how he develops his philosophical foundation for theology. Since he continues to influence theology through all of Christian history, we will have the occasion to return again and again to his thought. With this in mind we move forward.[19]

VII

The Harmony of Reason and Revelation in the Middle Ages

The topic of this chapter represents a particular emphasis. It is based upon the reading of Aquinas, whose thought I consider to be representative of a profound alternative to the Augustinian tradition. Of course, there were several other powerful options over the relation of reason and revelation, philosophy and theology. For example, the mystic tradition found a powerful exponent in Bonaventure, and there were Latin Averroists who exalted reason over revelation. At best this latter group insisted upon a principle of two-fold truth in which philosophy and theology had their separate provinces of knowledge and experience. But while Aquinas evaluated many sources, he took a distinctive position which is the subject-matter now before us.

The Problem of Religious Knowledge

The problem of religious knowledge was tackled by all of the Abrahamic religions, Christianity, Islam and Judaism, during the Middle Ages. One could assume that the historic conflicts during this period between these religions would have rendered any ecumenical exchange impossible. Happily, on the level of philosophical reflections these conflicts were transcended and all subsequent religious knowledge has been enriched by that fact. I shall attempt to show why this is so. There was an obvious cross-fertilization between leading thinkers of these Abrahamic religions as they struggled with epistemological issues during the medieval milieu. This assertion is confirmed in the writings of Averroes, Maimonides and Aquinas, among others.

Averroes

Ibn Rushd, known by his Latinized name (Averroes), was an Islamic philosopher of Cordoba in Spain. Averroes was mainly a philosopher of nature and a physician. He was not a member of the clergy or a theologian proper. This may account for his attraction to Aristotle, as well as his willingness to stand over against Islamic orthodoxy. He gave philosophy an exalted place in Islam, usually reserved for revelation in the Qur'an. Averroes wrote a series of commentaries on Aristotle which were to have wide-ranging as well as long-lasting influence. His tendency to advocate the primacy of reason over revelation led to his exile. But his influence lived on at the University of Paris. His ideas were to have a powerful and disturbing impact upon the Christian movement. A number of Christian scholars became Latinized followers of Averroes and exalted reason over faith in the manner in which they interpreted the Christian faith.[1]

From the beginning of his work, Averroes felt the pressure of the Islamic theologians to tone down his emphasis upon reason. His work entitled *The Agreement of Religion and Philosophy* was designed to reconcile philosophy and theology and thus soften the criticism aimed against his writing. But his attack on the writing of Al Gazali, the great saint, sage and mystic of Islam, was unfortunate. Al Gazali had asserted the primacy of faith over reason, especially in his *Destruction of the Philosophers*. Averroes answered Al Gazali in his *Destruction of the Destruction*, where reason and philosophy again assume the high ground. His fate was, therefore, sealed through banishment.

Maimonides

The Jewish philosophical tradition also made an impact on Christian theology during the Middle Ages. Moses Maimonides (1135–1204) was born in Cordoba as Moses ben Maimon. He left his home for north Africa in 1159. Settling near Cairo, he headed the Jewish community in Egypt. Maimonides was a physician as well as a philosopher. His scholarly work was intended to systematize and codify Jewish law. He is known as a thinker primarily through his famous book, *Guide for the Perplexed*. Maimonides was also a contemporary of Averroes. He seems to have been acquainted with the commentaries Averroes produced on Aristotle. There does not appear to have been any direct contact between the two philosophers. At the same time Aquinas read both Averroes and Maimonides critically, but maintained his own point of view.[2]

Aquinas will be our main concern in this chapter, as I have already indicated. I shall limit my interpretation of Aquinas to his theory of knowledge, with a bias toward his philosophical approach to theology rather than his theology proper. There can, however, be no clear distinction of these two disciplines in Aquinas, for Aquinas was a theologian who had a powerful intellect. Reason and revelation were interrelated in his pursuit of religious knowledge.

Before we turn to Aquinas, we will look briefly at his mentor, Albert Magnus or Albert the Great. It is through the interests and reflections of Albert the Great that we encounter some of the fundamental assumptions developed by Aquinas. This becomes very important for an in-depth appreciation of the enormous contribution of Aquinas as a philosopher and theologian of the Christian Faith.

Albert the Great

Albert was born in Lauingen in Swabia around 1206. He studied briefly at Bologna and Padua and then entered the Dominican order in 1223. Thereafter he taught in Germany and arrived in Paris in 1240 to study theology. There he taught theology from 1245–48. He was sent to Cologne in 1248 to organize the Dominican house of studies. It was here that Thomas Aquinas became his student. Albert lived mainly in Cologne, with visits to Rome, until his death in 1280.

Albert wrote on Peter Lombard, the Bible, Aristotle, Boethius, Pseudo-Dionysius and Averroes as well as producing a handbook on theology, *Summa Theologiae*. Albert was not a pure Aristotelian, but was greatly influenced by Aristotle. Ideas from Platonism, Neo-Platonism and Islamic philosophy filtered through his system of thought. Albert exalted Aristotle above Plato as a philosopher. But where he observed a conflict between philosophy and theology, he accepted the guidance of Augustine. In Albert, therefore, one observes Greek, Islamic and Christian influences. He saw this synthesis as being both possible and necessary from an intellectual point of view.[3]

Thomas Aquinas on the Harmony of Reason and Faith

We turn now to Aquinas, who is the main focus of this chapter. I have already observed that Aquinas was a student of Albert the Great. The fact that ideas may have flowed from Albert to Aquinas does not detract from the genius, creativity or unusual contribution of Aquinas to Christian thought. I would argue, however, that an examination of Albert enhances our initial understanding of the foundations of the system of Aquinas.

The Life of Aquinas

Thomas was born about 1224 at Roccasecca near Naples. His father was the Count of Aquino. Thomas studied at the University of Naples from 1239–1243. He entered the Dominican order in 1244. There is speculation that Thomas may have gone to Paris in 1245 to study with Albert. But he was the pupil of Albert later at the Dominican house of studies at Cologne from 1248 until he went to Paris in 1252. Thomas studied the Bible and the *Sentences* of Peter Lombard for about three years. In 1257, he was admitted to a professorship along with Bonaventure. During this early period of teaching, Thomas began his writing. Among these writings were: a commentary on the *Sentences*, two commentaries on Boethius (*On Being and Essence* and *On the Principles of Nature*), and a number of *Questions* (e.g. *On Truth*). He also began his work on the *Summa contra Gentiles* or *Summary* or *Manual Against the Gentiles*.

Returning to Italy about 1260, Aquinas taught at Orvieto, Rome and Viterbo. There he wrote the remainder of *Summa contra Gentiles*, some Bible commentaries, and began his famous *Summa Theologiae*. He wrote his *De potentia* or *On Power* and started a series of commentaries on Aristotle's writings.

In 1269, Thomas came back to Paris to continue his teaching at the university. He continued his writings and produced an important treatise *De Malo* (*On Evil*). He took part in the controversy between the theologians and the professors in the Faculty of Arts over the influence of Averroes. His work, *On the Unity of the Intellect Against the Paris Averroists* reflects this interest.

In 1272 Thomas went to Naples to found a Dominican house of studies in the university. While he was there, his writings on Aristotle and his *Summa Theologiae* continued. Early in 1274 he set out for Lyons, to take part in the work of the council. On this journey, he fell gravely ill and was not able to reach his destination.

It is obvious that Thomas was a frequent writer of profound insight and depth. He wrote profusely on scripture, theology and philosophy. He was aware of the widening of the intellectual outlook through the translations of Greek, Jewish and Islamic writings. It is to be remembered, however, that his main interest was that of a Christian theologian rather than to provide a synthesis of non-Christian thought and Christian belief.

Influences Upon His Thought

Aristotle was so central to Aquinas that some attention needs to be given to Aquinas's frequent use of Aristotle's thought. Aristotle, Thomas believed, provided a powerful instrument in the expression of a Christian world-view. Thomas was not interested in reconciling the two systems of thought: Aristotle's philosophy with Christian theology. He was interested, rather, in theological construction. For example, we might look briefly at the manner in which Aquinas used Aristotle's *Ethics*. Thomas saw the teleological ethics of Aristotle as a philosophical sub-structure for Christian ethics. When there was a conflict between Aristotle and his understanding of the Christian faith, Aquinas went with his faith. He believed, however, that truth from any source is to be honored. Christianity, according to Aquinas, can gain much from philosophical truth. It was his intention to use Aristotle's philosophy, which has so many worthy insights, as a means toward the systematic development of theology.

But Aquinas did not rely totally on Aristotle as his only non-Christian source. Aristotle was his philosopher *par excellence*, but it was philosophy in general which he sought to use as a means to rethink his ideas in order to forge a coherent system of thought. Augustine was a powerful influence upon Aquinas. It was also his direct encounter with Neo-Platonism, Islamic philosophy and Maimonides which broadened the base of his intellectual foundations.

If Aquinas borrowed so freely from many sources, we may question his originality. He was original in his ability to raise questions in new ways and present new lines of argumentation. He would on occasion reject a traditional view. He had the ability to sift through diverse opinions to get at truth and then weld ideas together systematically through the use of his vast knowledge of philosophical principles and categories. He did not simply adopt different ideas from a diversity of sources in order to juxtapose different philosophies. He insisted upon rethinking his materials coherently, critically and systematically, and with his theological mission in mind.

Thomas Aquinas was a professor of theology and therefore did not set out to construct a philosophical system. Even though the disciplines of philosophy and theology are closely associated in his thought, he was aware of a distinction between them. He held to certain revealed truths (i.e. the Trinity) which cannot be treated by means of philosophy. A theologian may, however, use philosophical concepts in the attempt to state such a belief in intellectual terms. There may be philosophical truths which are not revealed by God also. In the manner in which Aquinas presents his case, however, there does appear to be a limited overlapping of subject-matter. For example, let us look briefly at the existence of God.

Metaphysics proves, according to Aquinas, the existence of God; while God obviously is a theme for the theologian. The Bible, however, starts with the belief that God exists. Scripture presupposes God's existence as a matter of faith and goes on to deal with God's self-revelation and redemptive activity. The philosopher, on the contrary, starts with the objects of sense-perception, the things of this world, and arrives eventually at the knowledge of God's existence (in so far as inference will take such a thinker). Thus, if we start with Christian faith and explore its content and implications, we are thinking as theologians. If, on the other hand, we do not presuppose faith as a premise but rely solely on human reasoning, employing principles based on sense experience, we are thinking as philosophers.[4]

His Christian Philosophy

Aquinas presents what we may describe as a Christian philosophy. He was a person of faith before he became a philosopher. He was primarily a theologian who used philosophy for theological purposes. It is incorrect to assume that Aquinas turns to faith only after he exhausts all recourse to reason. Even the five arguments for the existence of God are attempts to demonstrate the existence of the God of theism in whom he already believed. The names he ascribes to God are also names of attributes of the personal God of the Bible. He mentions such attributes as knowledge, will, love, justice and mercy. When he treats problems of rational theology he often cites as authorities passages of the scriptures or the Fathers of the church. His demonstrations are what we may call rationalizations of his Christian beliefs. They are attempts to show that there are independent grounds for certain beliefs from selected characteristics of the world. In other words, they seek to show that a truth which has been reached by one route, revelation, can also be reached by another and quite a different route, reason. Although in his rational arguments as a philosopher he moves toward conclusions without any explicit reference to faith, his conclusions are those he has already accepted by faith.[5]

The Harmony of Reason and Revelation

In sum, Aquinas would state his position somewhat in the following manner: We begin by assuming that the Christian revelation is true. Evidence for this affirmation is found in the history of the Church, Aquinas believed. Now if God has truly spoken, the Christian revelation must be true and it is necessary for us to believe it. The purpose of revelation is to provide all, including philosophers, with the knowledge of God, of human nature and destiny and the means of salvation. Such knowledge has different elements. Aquinas was especially concerned with two classes of knowledge—reason and revelation.

First, there are revealed truths which, though they are revealed, are nevertheless attainable by reason alone. Such are, for instance, the existence of God and his essential attributes as well as the existence of the human soul and its immortality. God has revealed some truths which natural reason can attain, so that even metaphysicians might be saved. But since all are open to salvation, God enables each of us to know the whole saving truth immediately, with absolute certitude and perfect purity. Yet, any part of revelation which is attainable by natural reason should be considered rather as a necessary presupposition to matters of faith than as an article of faith proper. Only those persons who cannot see the truth of revelation in the light of reason are held in conscience to accept it by simple faith.

The second ground of revealed truths contains all the articles of faith properly said, that is to say, all of revelation which surpasses the range of reason. Such are, for example, the Trinity, the Incarnation and redemption. No philosophical speculation can provide the explanation of these truths. Philosophical conclusions cannot be deduced from such articles of faith. These are believed principles of equally believed theological consequences, and they are not intelligible principles of demonstrated rational conclusions. Reason cannot prove them to be true and it cannot prove them to be false.

On the contrary, to any sincere believer who is at the same time a true philosopher, the disparity between faith and reason becomes a sure sign that something is the matter with his philosophy. Faith is not a principle of philosophical knowledge, but it is a safe guide to rational truth as well as a warning against philosophical error. According to Aquinas, then, faith and reason grow into an organic unity because they both spring from the same source.[6]

VIII

Mysticism as Religious Knowledge

The Nature of Mysticism

Mysticism has sometimes been confused with pantheism, because they may co-exist. That is to say, some mystics have been pantheists and some pantheists have been mystics. Pantheism is the belief that God is everything and everything is God. Mysticism, on the other hand, is an experience of the divine, but it need not be associated with pantheism.

Mysticism Defined

Mysticism often arises when those who are theologically orthodox present a view of God which emphasizes God's transcendence to a point of virtually ignoring the immanence of God in the lives of humans. A good example of this tendency to exaggerate the transcendence of God is found in the thought of Aquinas. To Aquinas, God's perfection and immutability is so great that God is impassible. The vision of God, the highest good, cannot be attained in the present life. Even the medieval mystics refused to accept his judgment. Over against Aquinas, these mystics affirmed the immanence of God in the human soul. They also affirmed the possibility of the experience of blessedness in this world.

Mysticism may be divided into two categories: the outward or extrovert type and the inward or introvert type. The extrovert type looks outward through the senses, while the introvert type looks inward into the mind. The extrovert mystic, using the physical senses, perceives material objects—the sea, the sky, trees—mystically transfigured so that divine reality is revealed through them.

The introvert mystic, on the other hand, seeks to shut out the senses, by obliterating from consciousness the entire multiplicity of sensations, images and thoughts, to plunge into the depth of the ego. In darkness and silence, this latter mystic perceives the divine ultimate. The study of the thought of Meister Eckhart is instructive, since he brings together aspects of these two types of mysticism.[1]

A final preliminary concern presents itself before we turn to Eckhart. Mysticism can be associated with different understandings of the Ultimate. I use Ultimate here because mysticism is sometimes atheistic. It may be associated with monism, pantheism or theism as well. Atheistic mystics have as their goal the attainment of liberation of the self from evil or suffering into a state of fulfillment. Original Buddhism would appear to be a prime example of this manifestation.

Monistic Mysticism: Vedanta Hinduism

Monistic mysticism is illustrated in a powerful way in Hinduism, especially in the *Upanishads*. The ultimate was conceived as an impersonal cosmic principle, *Brahman*. This principle was identified with the Self, *Atman*, which was experienced in certain states in the depths of the human self. This *Brahman-Atman* was considered to be the Universal Self or the only true reality—"One without a second," while all else was understood as *Maya* or appearances. As long as one believes in the reality of these appearances and is ignorant of *Brahman-Atman*, the one true reality, one cannot escape from the wheel of birth and rebirth or *Samsara*. *Samsara* is tied to the cosmic law of cause and effect, *Karma*. *Karma* is the dreaded law of the deed. If one is to win liberation, *Moksha*, from the necessity of reincarnation, one must attain spiritual knowledge, *Vidya*, of *Brahman* as the only reality. This is the only knowledge capable of dispelling the illusory appearances of things. Only thus may one break the fetters which bind one to things and values of the spatio-temporal world. One can attain this spiritual knowledge by means of a vigorous physical and mental discipline, detaching oneself thereby from the things of the senses and meditating upon the sole reality, the *Brahman*. The culmination of this process is an intuitive realization of one's identity with *Brahman-Atman* through a mystical experience of union which brings with it peace and joy. This brief outline of a very involved system of thought is a convenient illustration of monistic mysticism.[2]

Theistic Mysticism: Judaism, Islam and Christianity

Theistic mysticism, on the contrary, rests upon belief in a personal God who is the Creator of nature and human life. This Creator-God is distinct from all finite persons and things. This form of mysticism seeks closeness to God through purification of the will as well as detachment from everything which binds us, the self to itself and to the world. The result of detachment from the world is an unclouded knowledge and vision of God together with a perfect love of the Divine Being. Theistic mysticism, when compared with monistic mysticism, does not deny the reality of finite things and selves. Nor is it necessary to hold that the individual self can attain identity with God.

Theistic mysticism has been characteristic of Semitic religions — Judaism, Islam and Christianity. Monistic mysticism has usually been associated with interpretations of Hinduism and Mahayana Buddhism. This radical contrast between mysticism East and West can be deceptive. For instance, theistic mysticism associated with Judaism, Christianity and Islam have often been influenced by Neo-Platonism and the mysticism associated with that source.

The Neo-Platonic Influence

In some cases Neo-Platonism has provided a type of mysticism which remains theistic, but has elements akin to monistic mysticism. A good example of this latter tendency is the thought of Meister Eckhart (1260–1327). Eckhart was a Dominican and a Scholastic. He was obviously influenced by Aquinas. But there was another powerful strand in his thought from Neo-Platonism mediated by Pseudo-Dionysius. This latter focus was radically different from the outlook of Aquinas. Eckhart was a synthetic but constructive thinker — an "intellectual" mystic. He was a theologian who lectured at both Paris and Cologne. Like Bernard of Clairvaux, Eckhart was a moving and effective preacher. He was an avid student of the New Testament and made use of its spirit and practical piety. Again, we observe Eckhart's involvement in practical activity as an administrator in his order. Eckhart combines several strands of thought in his system. His unique outlook combines Thomistic theology, Neo-Platonic philosophy and New Testament Christianity. This pattern of thought is brought together by his intellectual and spiritual genius.

Meister Eckhart's Theory of Knowledge

One faces great difficulty in interpreting Eckhart. We will limit our concern to that part of his system which illuminates his theory of knowledge.

Eckhart and Aquinas

One aspect of Eckhart's theory of knowledge depends heavily upon Thomism. For instance, both the natural order based on reason and the supernatural order grounded upon revelation are foundational to his system. As a mystic, however, Eckhart speaks in different terms. He asserts that the perfect knowledge of God is the result of God's activity within the depths of the human soul. The soul should be constant in its pursuit of this "unknowing knowing." Such knowledge is not based upon the senses or images through reasoning. This perfect knowledge sought by the mystic is "outward ignorance"—it provides no knowledge of external things. It provides us with knowledge of God. Thus as a mystic, Eckhart is closer to Neo-Platonism than to Thomism. We can enjoy, according to Eckhart, a direct experience of God in this life and do not have to be content with the knowledge about God attained from reason and revelation. But Eckhart is a Christian mystic rather than a follower of Plotinus. The knowledge of God cannot be attained by us through our own powers—it is a gift of God wrought by his activity in the soul.[3]

Like Aquinas, Eckhart distinguishes between the soul and its powers or faculties through which it acts. For example, when the soul understands it does so through the intellect. When it remembers, it does so through its memory. It loves through the will. The soul works with her powers and not with her essence. In addition to these higher powers of the soul, i.e. intellect, memory and will; there are lesser powers of the soul, i.e. sensation and desire. It is by means of the latter powers that the soul can relate to special and temporal realities.

Eckhart departs from Aquinas in the value he places upon the powers of the soul. According to Aquinas, grace perfects or builds upon nature. Aquinas, therefore, can ascribe a great deal of value to knowledge acquired by reason through the senses. Eckhart, on the other hand, sees any tendency to acquire knowledge through the senses as a negative factor. It distracts from perfect knowledge and a single-minded love of God. Here, Eckhart is closer to

Augustine. He is convinced that God is to be found within or at home in the soul. God is known in the ground of the soul when the powers of the soul have been brought to restand the soul is at rest — waiting on God.[4]

Eckhart does not seem to follow the prescribed stages of the mystical way — purgation, illumination and union.[5] He implies, instead, that one may experience mystical union directly after purgation of the soul by the withdrawal of its powers into its ground. Eckhart advocates *detachment* as a primary step to union. The soul is to be emptied in order to prepare for the divine entry. The emptiness of the soul is the pre-condition for a maximum capacity of divine manifestation within the soul. There must be absolute *stillness* and *passivity* within the soul. The human soul can contribute nothing by actions of its own to the speaking of God's word. It must surrender itself completely to God's action within it, if union is to take place.

Eckhart's Place in Christian Theology

Eckhart's mysticism presents problems for Christian theologians, because of the strong Neo-Platonic tendencies which we must now address. Neo-Platonic mysticism has *monistic* trends which are bothersome to Christian theologians. We find Neo-Platonic ideas in Eckhart's conception of God and his description of the soul's union with God. How may these elements be reconciled with the Christian focus of his thought?

We have observed that in Neo-Platonic thought (i.e. Plotinus) the ultimate reality is an impersonal One rather than the personal God of theism, generally characteristic of Christian theology. According to Plotinus, the world has emanated from this One, eternally and by necessity. The human soul, being weighted down by evils due to its association with matter, seeks to ascend back to its original source and attain union with the One. In this process the soul loses its consciousness (of itself) as a distinct being and unites with the One (the Good) in mystical ecstasy. In this union the One finds peace and joy. But the One is indescribable since it is an undifferentiated unity without quality or relation. Salvation is the flight of the alone (the human soul) to the Alone (God or One). This Neo-Platonic mysticism was mediated to Eckhart by such early medieval Christian thinkers as the Pseudo-Dionysius.

Eckhart makes a crucial distinction between *Deus*, "God," and *Deitas*, "Godhead." God refers to the personal God of Christian theism, including the Trinity. The soul, according to Eckhart, is not satisfied with union with God. It longs to find union with the Godhead—this is described as the eternal birth in the soul.

It is helpful to recall the thought of Plotinus as we seek to understand what Eckhart meant by "Godhead." God appears to imply what Plotinus meant by "Mind," while Godhead corresponds to the "One" in Plotinus' Godhead; it is Being itself and not an individual being. Godhead is, therefore, above all conceptions or comprehension. It is formless and without distinctions. It is eternal, indivisible, infinite and changeless. And yet these are negative statements which refer to a positive Reality. Being is pure knowledge, living and moving in itself.

Eckhart Compared with Brahmanism

Just as the One is above Mind in Plotinus, or *Brahman* is above *Isvara* in Sankara (a Hindu philosopher), so "Godhead" is above "God" in Eckhart. Godhead is the ultimate Ground of all being, flowing into all things and then flowing back into itself. Hence the soul is not content, according to Eckhart, to attain union with the personal, active and revealed God. It seeks union with the formless Ground which is behind and above God—plunging into the abyss of the Godhead. In this way Eckhart seeks language to express the incomprehensible, mysterious "otherness" of God. It is misleading to predicate personal or any other terms of God.[6] In some important aspects of his thought Eckhart anticipates Otto and Tillich.

Theism in Eckhart's Mysticism

It would be a mistake, however, to view Eckhart's position on the Godhead as equivalent to monistic mysticism. His intention is obviously theistic in the Christian sense. His metaphysical speculation concerning God rests upon a theistic foundation and is rooted in faith and piety. The self out of humility and trust seeks communion with God. It surrenders itself in obedience to God's will. God is experienced as merciful and forgiving love. Again, God is known as the source of new being and life in the soul. Eckhart's teaching about the birth of the Son in the soul is based upon a mystical interpretation of the union with Christ through the Holy Spirit. Thus in distinguishing "Godhead" from "God," Eckhart is not setting up a second, impersonal God. His God above God does not uproot the personal God of Christian theism. Eckhart's intention is to emphasize as a mystic the infinite and ineffable depths of God as we move beyond God's revelation to the essence of God in its hiddenness. According to Eckhart, God is also a consoling God. Mystical union immediately turns into a relationship of personal love, devotion and fellowship. Even "deification" does not mean "identification" with God. It implies a transfusion of self by God's Self or an entrance upon a new order of life, so harmonious with God that it can truly be said to be divine.[7] For Eckhart, the culmination of the mystical life is the transformation of the inner being of the self by love and the spontaneous expression of that being by works of love.[8]

In the quest for religious truth, mysticism represents a way of knowing which has its own characteristics over against intellection or reasoning. As we come to the close of our discussion on the medieval period of Christianity, it is appropriate for us to take a look at Eckhart, one of the greatest mystics of all times. Authentic mystics are rare, and especially those who combine a thirst for knowledge with high moral goals. Insight, the immediate apprehension of the inner nature of things or seeing reality intuitively, is the nature of knowledge related to authentic mysticism. Mystics often lay claim to a type of knowledge which is not sub-rational but supra-rational. The mystical experience is believed to make available to the seeker a knowledge of ultimate reality which is beyond the reach of the mind. In Eckhart, we have seen how one religious genius has worked this out.

IX

Knowledge and Faith in the Modern Period

Background to the Modern Period

The seventeenth century has been called the "age of genius." This is because several thought revolutions occurred during that century. Again, the results of earlier radical changes in thought took their effect in that period: the Renaissance, the Reformation, and the emergence of modern science.

A chain reaction of these several interacting forces created a climate in human thought which ripened into a revolution in religious thought as well as scientific discovery. The seventeenth century seemed to produce its share of persons of genius who were also willing to take the risk of persecution, if need be, to seek the truth wherever it would lead. Neither church authority nor Scholasticism were able to stem the flow of new ideas and the change in outlook which was to follow.[1]

The Renaissance

The Renaissance or the revival of learning in the fourteenth and fifteenth centuries was a time of rediscovery of knowledge. Scholasticism, in the service of the church, had driven much ancient wisdom underground. Church authority sponsored the views of the Schoolmen who favored Aristotle, but neglected a great deal of ancient wisdom. During the Renaissance, therefore, people rediscovered the broader heritage of ancient Greece and Rome. Reason in the form of human ability and dignity usurped the place of heavenly concerns and took the high ground. In fact, there was a tendency to turn away from metaphysics and theology and focus upon practical and earthly interests. Renaissance studies were known as the humanities. But they also included studies known today as the fine arts. The humanist was a well-rounded person. There was a disdain for scholarly work done in monasteries. Learning was a part of an active public life.

The Renaissance looked back in order to look forward. Hindsight was a means to foresight. The critical examination of ancient sources was to cast light upon the present and future. We may contrast this with the mind-set of the Medievalists, as we have mentioned above. The Renaissance person sought to put the ancient wisdom in perspective—it was the usable past for a new period of history. The revival of Platonic studies was one example of a return to the past for the sake of the future. Great progress was made in the return to the classics in many fields. The controlling purpose, however, was to seize new ideas and fresh investigations in the spirit of the age.

The Reformation

One way of viewing the Reformation is to see it as an attempt to recover the past in order to renew the church and society in the present. When we take this perspective, we discover Erasmus as well as Luther and Calvin. All these persons reacted against the authority of medieval scholasticism and went back to earlier sources. Whereas Luther and Calvin stressed mainly the biblical and theological roots of the Reformation, Erasmus mined the ancient classical sources as well. The place of Erasmus, much overlooked in Reformation studies, is that of a vital bridge between Renaissance and Reformation studies.

Erasmus, Luther and Calvin, among others, sought the roots of the historic faith in the first centuries of the church. For example, they went behind Aquinas to Augustine. Again, they rejected the reign of Aristotle, philosophically, and adopted much of the Neo-Platonic style.

For the Reformers, the Bible became the primary source of faith. They accepted its authority with a personal trust. But at the same time they examined biblical texts critically with the tools of Renaissance scholarship. Erasmus was a loyal Catholic, but he provided Luther and Calvin with a Greek New Testament. This meant that the Latin Vulgate of the medieval church was no longer normative. Luther translated the Bible into German. Calvin applied Renaissance scholarship to law and government as well as to the

Bible and theological knowledge. And he examined the Bible in its historical and cultural contexts as he looked for the original intentions of the biblical writers.

The printing press was invented to publish the Bible. This revolutionized human life. It aided considerably the rapid spread of information. The Gutenburg Bible was printed in 1454. Published works provided people with new ideas and independence from authorities. A period of criticism of church and society, through the printed word, ensued.

The Scientific Revolution

The modern world-view began in earnest in the seventeenth century. This is not merely true of theology; the same can be said of philosophy and natural science. I shall therefore classify the "modern" period as the seventeenth and eighteenth centuries and the "contemporary" period as the nineteenth and twentieth centuries. I am aware that such a classification is somewhat arbitrary. It does, however, provide a framework for our discussion, which is helpful.

There were at least two discoveries toward the close of the Renaissance and Reformation which helped to shape the modern period of thought.

First, there was the development of modern mathematics by Christopher Clarius (1537–1612), often called the modern Euclid. According to Clarius, mathematical demonstrations are superior to dialectical disputations. This belief that mathematics is a fundamental science which renders truth certain aided the development of philosophical rationalism in the following centuries. Rationalism was Platonism pushed to its extreme. It emphasized "innate ideas" and the ability to deduce all other knowledge from them. It is likewise obvious that this new mindset is the basis for modern natural science.

Second, there was the introduction of exact methods of experimentation and observation. This is especially true of the telescope developed by Galileo (1564–1642). Through it he saw with his own eyes that the earth rotated around the sun and that there were mountains on the moon. Both observations contradicted long and firmly held assumptions grounded in the statements of ancient authorities—both scripture and tradition.

A new method emerged which represented a decisive break with the past. Galileo did not consult the authorities—he looked! New knowledge flowed from experiments which opened up the possibilities for modern science. In philosophy, this pointed the way to eighteenth-century empiricism. Empiricism looked back and looked forward. It developed one side of Aristotle, but not the Aristotle of the Schoolmen. Its stress was on sense data as a primary source of information from which all other knowledge could be validly induced.

Rationalism

The Rationalism of the seventeenth century was developed by Descartes (French), Spinoza (Dutch) and Leibniz (German). Since Spinoza and Leibniz built upon the foundation laid by Rene Descartes, we shall briefly introduce the others, but lift Descartes up for fuller treatment.

Baruch Spinoza (1632–1677) was a Dutch Jew who made his living grinding lenses. Descartes had left behind a significant problem on which he worked. Mind and body appeared to be two separate and incompatible substances. How did they function together? Spinoza accepted Descartes' mathematical model for synthesizing all knowledge into one system. Spinoza went on to tighten its systematic consistency by insisting that there is but one substance (in two aspects—thought and extension). The one *divine* substance he sometimes called *God* and sometimes called *Nature*. Spinoza is a monist, who may be considered either as an atheist or as a "God-intoxicated" man, depending upon which dimension of his system is being considered as normative.

Gottfried Wilhelm Leibniz (1646–1716) was a son of a university professor at Leipzig. He was educated at Leipzig, studied philosophy and travelled extensively. Leibniz is said to have met Sir Isaac Newton and Spinoza. He was known as a mathematician, scientist, historian, diplomat, theologian and philosopher. Leibniz was involved in many pursuits. Thus much of his philosophy is to be found in letters, memoranda and articles. He had a great deal in common with Descartes and Spinoza.

Leibniz hoped to systematize all conceivable knowledge in a rational scheme consistent with the principles and certainty of mathematics. His program was to accomplish two things: First, he sought a perfect universal scientific language that would reduce all thoughts to mathematical symbols. Second, he developed calculus. Here Leibniz is similar in his pursuit to Isaac Newton, but he appears to have worked independently.

It was Leibniz's intention to bring all thought under the control of symbolic logic. He is known for his thesis of "pre-established harmony" as well as his assertion that this is the "best possible of all worlds" (theodicy). Furthermore, he reclaims some of the atomism of Lucretius in his monadic theory of the universe. The thought Leibniz stimulated in science, philosophy and theology is considerable.

Empiricism

Rationalism did not succeed in solving many issues of ultimate concern, during its reign in the seventeenth century. Thus in the eighteenth century empiricism arose as a possible alternative.

In Great Britain this new philosophical movement was growing. The continental movement (rationalism) had stressed the mathematical side. The British movement, on the other hand, emphasized the side of observation and experiment. It was characterized by an *empirical* and *inductive* approach to knowledge. All knowledge was said to be acquired by induction from sense experience alone.

Isaac Newton was the scientist-mathematician of the British movement. The philosophers were: Locke (English), Berkeley (Irish) and Hume (Scottish). We shall look briefly at Newton, Locke and Berkeley, and select Hume for more thorough examination.

In science and mathematics, Sir Isaac Newton led the way. Newton was born in 1642, the year Galileo died. He elaborated the essentials of calculus and discovered that white light is the presence of all colors. His most important achievement was to grasp the principle of gravity.

Newton wrote his *Mathematical Principles of Natural Philosophy* in 1687. His ideas were associated with the emergence of the Age of Enlightenment. It was believed that humans had come of age: that we will be able to solve all of our problems through human intelligence. The method of observation and experimentation took charge.

Following Newton's lead, three British philosophers set out to develop the empirical method. These were Locke, Berkeley and Hume. For more than a century these thinkers (and others influenced by them) attempted to work out the metaphysical and epistemological implications of Newtonian science. They found knowledge to be based on what could be derived by induction from sense experience.

John Locke (1632–1704) took an approach almost opposite to Descartes. At birth, according to Locke, our mind is a *tabula rasa*,

a blank tablet. All of our ideas originate in sense experience. Ideas
come from outside the mind. According to Locke, matter causes
sensations. Matter was understood to be the stuff external to us that
had power to cause sensations received by our sight, hearing, taste,
touch and smell.

George Berkeley (1685–1753) was disturbed by Locke's deistic
God. In fact, he took exception to much that Locke had said. He
therefore sought a different method. He reasoned that if people
believed that the source of all our ideas was inert, unthinking matter,
they would become materialists, even atheists. Berkeley was also a
devoted empiricist, but he approached the subject from a different
angle of vision. He insisted that the nature of our experience
indicates that no idea exists in human experience unless it exists as
perceived by some mind. He goes on to assert that the only mind
capable of causing all the richness and diversity that we experience
with our senses is the mind of God. It is *God*, therefore, and not
matter that causes sensations. God, according to Berkeley, is the
only sufficient source or cause of all sensations and ideas everywhere.

Having looked at several collaborators in the rationalism and
empiricism of the modern period, we now take up with greater
intensity three representative thinkers. Descartes set the stage
for Rationalism. Hume was perhaps the greatest of the British
Empiricists, especially in his arousal of Kant. It was Kant who
attempted, in his critical philosophy, to synthesize rationalism and
empiricism in his system. All of these thinkers had a profound
impact upon theology as well as philosophy. They therefore have
an important place in our discussion on the impact of philosophy
upon theology.[2]

The Cartesian Method

We turn now to René Descartes and his theory of knowledge.
Descartes, a central figure in the "scientific revolution" of the
seventeenth century, was born in 1596. This was fifty years after
Copernicus had proposed that the earth rotates daily on its axis and
revolves yearly about a central sun. He died in 1650, some forty
years before Newton's formulation of the laws of mechanics and
universal gravitation. In other words, his generation was pivotal to
the transition from the medieval world to the modern period of
science, philosophy and theology. Descartes and his contemporaries
participated largely in this period of transition.[3]

Astronomy was the science that set the pace for the advances in the early seventeenth century. In 1610 Galileo did his work. His observations, already mentioned, proved to be an insurmountable obstacle to the Ptolemaic earth-centered model of the universe, and shattered the Aristotelian-Ptolemaic cosmology. Descartes was to echo Galileo's assertion that mathematics is the key to grasping the nature of reality. The language essential to understanding the "book of the universe" was mathematics. It was the mathematical skills of Kepler that enabled him to develop his theory that the planets move in elliptical as opposed to circular orbits. Descartes himself produced *Optics*, in which he discussed the problems of telescope design. In 1620, Francis Bacon published his *Novum Organon*, in which he put forward a set of precepts for the investigation of natural phenomena and their causes. Bacon's new method of induction aided empirical research in the struggle to understand the universe. Descartes came upon the scene amidst a growing awareness of the importance of conducting experiments and observation in the quest for knowledge. It would be his role to establish the philosophical foundation to undergird the growing scientific revolution.

Descartes did his work at a time when the attainment of knowledge was considered difficult. It was associated with occult powers and forces. The acquisition of knowledge was also controlled and restricted by religious authority and theological beliefs. Descartes was convinced that he had as his destiny the founding of a new philosophical system. This mission, as he saw it, was not mysterious and did not depend upon superhuman intellectual endowments. Descartes saw knowledge as a very simple thing. He insisted that truth is readily accessible by the ordinary human intellect. True knowledge is open rather than hidden, simple rather than complex, clear and certain rather than full of doubt.

Early in his writings, Descartes asserted that philosophical knowledge has three main features: *unity, purity* and *certainty*.

Descartes rejected the scholastic conception of science as a set of separate disciplines, each with its own methods and level of precision. The separatist view claimed the authority of Aristotle. Descartes appears to have reverted to the Platonic notion of philosophy as a unified system. In his view, the various elements of the system are coherent and inter-linked as a set of theorems in mathematics. All things which fall under the category of human knowledge are interconnected, and each link in a long chain is simple and easily understood.

Descartes sought a system free of any taint of falsity. *Purity* was the second characteristic of true knowledge. As he observed the prevailing doctrines, they appeared to contain some elements of truth, but this truth was corrupted by a large mixture of incoherence and inaccuracy. He looked to mathematics, especially arithmetic and geometry, to illustrate an expression of purity of truth. These sciences make no assumptions that experience might render uncertain—they are pure and simple. The high standards characteristic of mathematics were a constant inspiration for Descartes as he did his philosophical work.

The notion of *certainty* is perhaps the most important characteristic of true knowledge for Descartes. In ordinary usage we may know something without claiming absolute certainty for its truth. Descartes considers philosophy as of a higher order than an ordinary quest after truth. The philosopher, in his view, is the seeker after wisdom or understanding—one who desires a level of knowledge that is above the ordinary. Descartes begins by offering intuition as the basis for acquiring certain knowledge. It is through *lumen naturale*, "the light of nature," or *lux rationis*, "natural light," that we arrive at self-evident truth by means of *intueri*, intuition. But this approach left serious questions. How does one go beyond mathematics? How does one treat complicated issues? And, how does one direct intuition when it does not hit its target?

This independence from intuition is manifested in Descartes's earliest major work, *Regulae*, or *Rules for the Direction of the Understanding*. About a decade later, he seems to have grasped the difficulties involved in the search for true knowledge. He provides more details and plots out a plan in this pursuit. He suggests an orderly manner of seeking knowledge by direction of thought—beginning with the simplest and most easily known objects and ascending little by little to more complex levels of knowledge. In his famous *Discourse on Method* he outlines a new and much more dynamic philosophical approach, the method of doubt. He goes on to show how the systematic rejection of beliefs which are open even to the slightest doubt can serve as a vehicle for the discovery of a reliable starting point in philosophy.

Method was central to Descartes and his system of thought. He decided to doubt everything he had ever learned until he came to some clear and evident idea, a first principle, that could not be doubted. He came to the conclusion that he could not doubt that he was doubting. If he was *doubting*, then he was *thinking*. And if he was thinking, then he existed as a thinking being. His first principle, therefore, became, *je pense, donc je suis*, "I am thinking, therefore I exist." The Latin formulation, *cogito, ergo sum*, is more familiar. According to Descartes, human nature is basically mind, to which body is attached. Rationality is the key to reality. Through this method, associated in his thinking with mathematical certainty, Descartes believed that he could come to certain knowledge of everything. He began with an idea within himself that seemed obvious to his reason. Then by rational deduction he went on to demonstrate the existence of everything including God and the world. Through his world-view and by his philosophical method, he initiated an outlook based upon the proper use of the mind as the basis for all true knowledge. This Cartesian perspective was soon to influence science and theology as well as philosophy. This was the problem that Spinoza, Leibniz and even Kant would tackle.

David Hume's Theory of Knowledge

The skepticism of David Hume (1711–1776) has had a powerful effect on the course of religious thought since his time. It questioned the attempt of philosophers to demonstrate religious truths such as the existence of God and immortality. During his youth, Hume lost interest in the Calvinist teachings of his native Scotland. These teachings were grim, austere and gloomy. Superstitions and fanaticism made the situation more hopeless. At an early age, therefore, Hume abandoned the whole of Calvinist doctrine. Unfortunately, he appears to have equated Calvinism with religion in general. Thus his aversion of Calvinism, as he knew it, affected his attitude toward religion in any form. And yet, intellectually, he continued to be interested in religion for all of his life. Religion was more a subject for investigation. It was something he observed in others and in society—it was not something that informed his life or personal convictions. Hume seemed to be at home in the cultural world of Edinburgh. He did not appear to be disturbed by sin and had no sense of need for divine aid. It was his view that popular religion is irrational; it perverts and weakens all of intellectual and moral life.

Hume's major influence as a skeptic is not related to his attacks upon "popular" religion; it is rather his criticism of "natural" religion. Having dismissed revealed religion, he focused his attention upon the religion of reason. During the Age of Reason, this version of religion was founded upon the scientific view of nature developed, in Britain, by Newton. According to this view, God had created the world and imposed order upon it by means of immutable laws. Since the order of nature is God's handiwork and a product of God's intelligence, it constitutes a revelation of God's power and wisdom. This Newtonian picture of the universe was accepted widely in the Britain of the eighteenth century. A teleological argument for God's existence stemmed from it which was somewhat different from that which was inherent in the cosmological argument of Aquinas. It is the Newtonian argument with which Hume is primarily concerned in his *Dialogues Concerning Natural Religion*.

As we have seen, two directions resulted from the scientific method stemming from Kepler, Copernicus and Galileo. These were the rationalist and empiricist movements. The first was known as continental rationalism, espoused by such thinkers as Descartes, Spinoza and Leibniz. We are now concerned with the second direction of the scientific revolution which developed in the British environment. The scientific method took on an empirical trend and emphasized observation and experimentation. Newton stood at the fountainhead of this empiricist movement. He was a mathematician, but insisted upon verification of his physical theories by an appeal to sense experience. This had a decisive effect upon British empiricist philosophers, like Locke and Hume.

The empiricists asserted that knowledge originates not in self-evident reason but from experience, and that even the most complex ideas are derived from what Locke called "simple ideas" of "sensation" and "reflection" by a process of comparison and composition. This empiricist view questioned the validity of metaphysical speculation by abstract reasoning. It insisted upon testing the meaning and truth of every general idea by tracing it back to its origin in experience.

Hume carries the empirical theory of knowledge to extremes. He reacted to Locke and Berkeley, but disagreed with both. He accepted Locke's conclusion that there are no innate ideas, and that all ideas in our minds come from our senses. But when asked "What causes our sensations?" Hume said, "We don't know!" All we know, based upon sense experience, is that we do have sensations. Hume attempts to show that many metaphysical speculations have no grounding in experience. He insists that it is from sense experience alone that we have knowledge. And based upon this assertion, we do not know with certainty that cause and effect are connected, that there is an external world, a self, or God. All ideas could be explained psychologically. By custom or habit, we associate ideas with experiences where there is no connection which can be demonstrated. Hume asserts that we may retain our beliefs for practical purposes, if we wish to do so. But as philosophers we should be honest enough to admit that empirically we know almost nothing.

Hume raised some lasting issues in philosophy and theology. It was his challenge to the important beliefs of the Christian faith that stimulated profound reflection. We must appreciate his thought in itself. But equally important is the fact that he stimulated the mind of Kant, who used all of his genius to respond to the profound issues raised by Hume.

Kant and His Problem

Immanuel Kant (1724–1804) attempted to bring the rationalism of the Continent and the empiricism of Britain together. This, however, was no easy task. This is why the genius of this giant intellect is so evident in Kant's critical philosophy.

Kant was born in Königsberg, Germany. He travelled little and remained close to home. He was an ivory-tower bachelor lost in his books. But his thought revolutionized metaphysics, ethics and theology. We still must grapple with problems he raised.

Kant was influenced by Christian Wolff, who transmitted the tradition of Descartes and Leibniz. It was his study of David Hume that "awakened him from his dogmatic slumber." Kant read Rousseau avidly. In Rousseau, Kant was introduced to feeling and conscience. This was something absent in both logical arguments and sensory experience.

In his philosophy, Kant seeks to reconcile the scientific view of nature formulated by Newton with his own profound convictions, derived largely from Christianity. He held the conviction that there is a moral order which transcends the world of the senses. On the one hand, he had a profound interest in the sciences and accepted the dominant Newtonian conception of nature, which he had encountered at his university at the age of sixteen. On the other, he was deeply affected by Pietism in his family and early study. German Pietism emphasized moral earnestness and strict discipline. It stressed the urgency of the moral law written upon the heart. It pointed to the radical evil in human nature and the need for a complete change of orientation to attain the good life. Pietism had a permanent and positive impact on Kant. And yet, because of the critical nature of his mind he could not accept fanaticism or moral hypocrisy. Thus, there develops a conflict in his mind between his Christian piety and the scientific view of the world. It is to his credit that he held on to the fundamental beliefs of an ethical theism throughout his life. A strong challenge to him was to find a way to belief that could be reconciled with modern science.

Kant wanted to know how knowledge is possible. He set out to provide a *transcendental* critique of human knowing. By *transcendental*, Kant meant something which did not reside in human experience, but made human experience possible. His transcendental critique sought for the *a priori* (prior to experience) conditions in the mind itself that made knowledge possible.

According to Kant, rationalism and empiricism are at once partly right, but are limited and dependent upon each other. Empiricism is correct in the assumption that the material of our knowledge comes from the senses. If we had no sense data, we would have no knowledge. But rationalism has the advantage when it insists that the form of knowledge was supplied by the mind. Kant argues that we could have no knowledge if certain categories of our minds failed to give meaningful shape to the data that the senses provide.

Kant sees no problem concerning the possibility of *a priori analytic* judgments. Such judgments are those in which the predicate merely explicates the subject without adding anything to it. They depend for their truth upon the law of contradiction, since their denial involves a logical contradiction. His problem, therefore, is limited to the possibility of *synthetic* judgments, or those judgments in which the predicate amplifies the subject and extends our knowledge.

According to Kant, mathematics, natural science and metaphysics consist of propositions which are not only *a priori* but also *synthetic*. Such judgments do not arise from our experience, and yet they add something to our knowledge. For instance, the judgment that 5 + 7 = 12, or the judgment in physics that "every event has a cause," is a *synthetic a priori* judgment. This is so since in neither case can the predicate be found by analysis of the subject (to be contained in the subject). Kant's problem can be expressed in these questions: How are synthetic judgments *a priori* possible? How are such judgments possible in mathematics, natural science and metaphysics?

Kant's response is a type of "Copernican revolution" in epistemology. His theory of knowledge begins with the bold assertion that for objects to be known they must conform to the mind, not the mind to objects. He assumes that the mind is active rather than passive in the process of knowing and that it adds something of its own. The *content* of our knowledge is derived from sense experience; the *form* is imposed by reason, and this provides the *a priori* element in knowledge. Our knowledge has two sources: *sensibility* and *understanding*. First, we have the capacity to receive impressions. Second, we have the power to know an object through these representations. The object is given to us through sensibility. It is *thought* in relation to what is given and that is understanding. Thus, without sensibility no object would be given. Without understanding no object would be thought. Thoughts without content are empty, and intuitions without concepts are nonsensical or blind. In order, therefore, to respond to the question of synthetic *a priori* judgments it is necessary to analyze sensibility and understanding further.

An analysis of sensibility discloses that although it is a faculty of receptivity through which objects are presented to us by means of impressions, it also contains certain forms of intuition, i.e. *space* and *time*. Sensibility imposes these types of impressions upon its object. It is therefore impossible for us to experience objects except as they conform to space and time as forms of our sensibility. Our sense impressions are ordered in relation to one another in space and they occur in succession to one another in time. But they are ordered in these ways, not because space and time are objective realities in which objects are located and events occur, but because they are subjective forms which we bring with us to all sense experience. In this manner we are able to relate our impressions to one another. Thus, we see how *a priori* forms of intuition belong to our sensibilities.

At the same time, the understanding, as a faculty of thought, affects the object thought, for example, through its categories of *substance* and *cause*. It is through substance and cause that the understanding is able to relate its manifold sense impressions to one another and organize them into a coherent whole of objects of experience. The categories are not "innate ideas." They are, rather, forms of synthesis belonging to our understanding and brought into play when impressions are presented to it by our sensibility.

According to Kant, it is by means of these categories and the principles of understanding through which they are applied to sense impressions that it becomes possible to experience objects in space and time as a coherent and organized whole. These categories and principles are *a priori*. It is through these entities that understanding expresses itself as a synthesizing faculty, as it thinks upon all objects presented to it. We able to know in advance the general form which all objects of experience must take. Understanding can think them only by imposing its character upon them and making them conform to its structure. The content of our knowledge of objects, however, cannot be anticipated, but must come to us through experience.

There is a constructive result from the critical examination of sensibility and understanding. Synthetic *a priori* judgments of mathematics and natural science are possible as forms of sensibility and categories and principles of understanding are imposed by reason upon impressions.

But there is a reverse impact in Kant's reflection. His negative conclusion has had a profound impact upon metaphysics and theology. Since space and time and the categories are applicable only to objects presented by the intuition of the senses, we can have knowledge only of things as they appear to us, *phenomena*. On the other hand, "things-in-themselves," *noumena*, are beyond our capacity to know. If we had the power of non-sensual or intellectual intuition, it could be possible for "things-in-themselves" to be presented to us and be known by reason. But this is not the case. We lack such power. Sensible objects, therefore, can be known through reason, while supersensible objects cannot — the latter are beyond the reach of reason.

Kant, however, leaves room for objects beyond sense and the reach of reason: "things-in-themselves." There are at least two reasons for this. First, it is necessary to account for that which is given in experience. Second, reason possesses certain "Ideas," such as freedom and God, which do not correspond to objects in the world of phenomena, but which suggest transcendent objects in the world behind phenomena. On the one hand, sensibility and understanding make mathematical and scientific knowledge of the sensible world of phenomena possible. On the other hand, reason can know only *that* there are "things-in-themselves" beyond phenomena; it cannot know *what* they are.

Epistemology was pushed to center stage in Kant's critical philosophy. The question is not "What do we know?" It is "How do we know?" We no longer ask how knowledge could conform to the nature of objects outside ourselves. Now, said Kant, *we make nature!* Nature was understood as a system of objects manifesting an order on which predictions could be based. Kant contended that the human mind provided that order. Objects, therefore, conformed to human understanding. Yet, knowledge was objective because all people's minds were structured so as to order the same sense data into identical patterns.

According to Kant, there is also a *noumenal world*—a world outside human sense experience. Kant wanted objective knowledge in the moral realm as well as in the scientific. For Kant the realm of human values is more important than the realm of nature. But one cannot acquire the knowledge of moral values either from reason or sense experience. Knowledge of the noumenal world lies inside the individual. Morality is a postulate of the *practical reason*. All people have within, Kant believed, a sense of *oughtness* that rightly guides them. This he designated the *categorical imperative*. On the basis of this "inner sense," people could obtain a practical certainty of *a rational faith* which assures the existence of God, freedom of choice and immortality. Thus, the faith which Kant uproots through *pure reason* is brought back and secured through *practical reason*.

Kant in this manner attempted to reconcile the mechanistic view of modern science with the view based upon empirical evidence. The mechanistic view of modern science rightly applied to the world of appearances. Empirical evidence and mathematical reasoning enabled people to understand and, to some extent, control the world as they perceived it. At the same time, Kant was able to hold to a belief in human freedom and moral responsibility that exempted humans from being just another cog in the cause-and-effect chain of natural science. Humans belong to two worlds, the phenomenal and the noumenal.

Descartes, Hume and Kant and the Future of Religious Thought

In this chapter I have provided the historical context of the modern period of religious thought in the West. After looking at several movements and persons who set the stage for this period, I treated the thought of Descartes, Hume and Kant with more intensity. I presented Descartes as the mind behind the scientific and rationalistic tendencies of the time. Sir Isaac Newton was mentioned as the natural scientist and mathematician who helped to shape the worldview of the modern period. However, it was Hume, the radical empiricist and religious skeptic, who as a philosopher raised the issues to a crisis level. It was Hume, as we have seen, who stimulated the mind of Kant to struggle with concerns raised by the rationalists on the continent and the empiricists in Britain. And it is through

Kant's critical philosophy that many problems raised during that period are still under investigation in philosophy, ethics and theology.

X

Contemporary Religious Thought (I): The Nineteenth Century

Issues in the Nineteenth Century

A Climate of Progress

The nineteenth century has been called the Age of Progress. By the mid-century there were, however, several political conflicts in France, Germany, Austria, Italy and Hungary. The United States was soon plunged into a Civil War. Yet in spite of these crises, a spirit of optimism was present. England was sufficiently quiet to lead this upbeat outlook.

Queen Victoria was on the throne. About 1851 a Great Exhibition was held in England. The theme of this display was "Progress," and the purpose of it was to unveil the works of industry of all nations. It attracted more than six million viewers. There was a display of raw materials, manufactured goods and great machines—i.e. locomotives, hydraulic presses, power looms, etc.

This splendid display was designed to illustrate the progress made in a half-century. At the beginning of the nineteenth century the majority of all Europeans lived on farms. Tools were made by hand. Power came from the wind and water as well as human and animal labor. Travel was mainly by horse or ship. But by mid-century machines were providing transport, power and manufacture. Concurrent with this change, there was a population shift from rural to urban life. The revolution that England celebrated was the Industrial Revolution. The gradual change of several centuries suddenly erupted with full force in the nineteenth century. It was deemed worthy of celebration. Hence the Great Exhibit called "Progress."

As those who observe the close affinity between thought and

action, we are to be reminded, at once, of two important thinkers. Karl Marx sat in the British Museum Library researching and writing his critique of capitalism. In Denmark, Søren Kierkegaard deplored the conformity of most people to the dictates of the state and church. The former was to cast significant light upon our collective existence, especially in reference to the political economy. The latter was to explore our individual existence, especially the ethical and theological significance of life. At the same time, most Victorians were enchanted over the promised future of progress.

In philosophy, the natural sciences, technology, as well as in the behavioral sciences, it was as if a dike had been broken open and the flood of human genius of many centuries had gushed forth. Technological developments from the mid-century until the outbreak of World War I (1914) changed the world-view and lifestyle in all countries where such changes were manifest. The telephone, the street light, the camera, and many other inventions were transformative. Louis Pasteur and others made discoveries to make surgery safer and the art of medicine more effective. Industrialists were perfecting ways to make steel, aluminum, combustion engines, dynamite and machine guns. In 1903 Henry Ford established his first factory and the Wright Brothers made their first flight in an airplane.

With breakthroughs in scientific theory there was a new era of thought and application. In physics, Einstein developed his theory of relativity, while Mark Planck formulated quantum mechanics. In mathematics attempts were made to found a universal algebra, forging beyond Euclidean geometry. Between 1910 and 1913, Bertrand Russell and Alfred North Whitehead co-authored a work entitled *Principia Mathematica*. In this work, Russell and Whitehead attempted to demonstrate that all mathematics could be deduced from a few principles of formal logic. Their work caused ferment in an area that had been rather constant since Aristotle.

In the second half of the century the social sciences also blossomed. Sigmund Freud was born in 1856 and Emile Durkheim in 1858. Their names are identified with psychology and sociology. Anthropology arose as a systematic study of pre-literate human societies. Archaeologists unearthed artifacts of past human civilizations all over the globe. There was literally a knowledge explosion in many fields.

A positive attitude toward change was the new intellectual element in the nineteenth century. In 1867, the British Prime Minister, Benjamin Disraeli, captured the sentiment of the hour in his insistence that, in a progressive society, change is constant and inevitable. Charles Darwin published his *Origin of Species* in 1859. This was an influential and controversial book, which still divides the minds of religious people. By the end of the nineteenth century, most scientists accepted some version of the evolutionary hypothesis. And yet, from its introduction, some non-scientifically educated people saw the idea of evolution as a major threat to biblical and ethical authority. Several ministers and theologians were among the opponents to evolution. Others saw its benefits—it guaranteed human progress and was a source of enlightenment regarding natural phenomena. They pointed to developments in science, medicine and technology to support their affirmative stance.

Philosophers of Progress

It is not surprising that the nineteenth century produced several philosophers of progress. We shall look briefly at one such philosopher in the English-speaking world, John Stuart Mill (1806–1873).

In his social and political philosophy, Mill stressed the importance of human freedom and the development of strong individual character. In ethics, he was a strong advocate of Utilitarianism, a position which stressed the greatest good for the greatest number of people. He is said to have been in favor of the equality of women. Religiously, Mill concluded that skepticism was the proper religious attitude toward supernatural religion. He believed in a limited deity with whom humans could cooperate to bring about improvements in the world.

There were several philosophers of *process* and *becoming* in Europe and America. Herbert Spencer (1820–1903) popularized Darwin's views in the behavioral sciences. Henri Bergson (1859–1941) wrote of a vital force (*élan vital*) that guided unceasing evolution and could be known by intuition and instinct. The poet William Wordsworth inspired people with a sense of change as well as human continuity with nature. Empiricism and pragmatism were presented by William James (1842–1910). John Dewey (1859–1952) built on James' work and applied it especially to American education.

Hegel and Idealism

The Idealism of Hegel had a profound influence upon European and American philosophy, at least until World War I, which is considered as the event that brought the nineteenth century to a close (in 1914). G. W. F. Hegel (1770–1831) had a decisive influence on Bradley and Royce. He also influenced Kierkegaard, negatively, while his impact upon Marx is often noted. Thus Hegel's influence upon the philosophy and theology of the nineteenth century was seminal in a profound sense and will be briefly treated here.

At a time when reason has been dethroned in religious circles, it is important to consider Hegel's contribution. Hegel's thought is a classic statement of an idealistic interpretation of philosophy in the West. In some ways his views correspond to the monistic religious philosophy of the East, especially the Advaita philosophy of the Hindu philosopher, Sankara.

Hegel's *Logic* examined the concepts and categories developed by human reason as a means of interpreting experience. Hegel is post-Kantian, as he refused to limit the interpretation of human experience by the categories which Kant had set up. Logic, according to Hegel, is not limited to the *form* of thought. It is also interested in its *content*. The analysis which logic provides goes beyond the mere analysis of the categories involved in thinking. Logic is likewise concerned with an analysis of metaphysical theories in relation to the different categories they employ as keys to the interpretation of reality as a whole.

According to Hegel, substance is a category which must be treated as "subject"—it is a spiritual reality capable of self-determination, freedom, creativity and purpose. Reason moves from the lower to the higher, from abstract to concrete, categories of thought and metaphysical interpretations of reality. The movement, therefore, culminates in the "Absolute Idea" or "Spirit," which is the highest category and as such the key to reality as a whole.

The method by which reason moves from the lower to the higher categories of thought is *dialectic*. The dialectic method has positive value for Hegel. It reflects the tensions of opposites in reality and discovers behind these tensions an underlying unity. A thesis is advanced, but when it is critically examined it shows its one-sidedness. One then encounters its opposite, its antithesis, which in turn discloses its inadequacy. Reason goes beyond both the thesis and antithesis to a synthesis which sets them aside but at the same time preserves the truth in each of them. They are annulled (*aufgehoben*), but taken up into a more concrete and adequate view of the synthesis. Reason, therefore, moves through one conflict of opposites after another to higher and higher categories until it reaches the highest, the "Absolute Idea."

The relation between understanding (*Verstand*) and reason (*Vernunft*) in Hegel differs from Kant. Kant insisted that reason is incapable of forging beyond knowledge of phenomena to a knowledge of *noumena*, things-in-themselves. But, according to Hegel, reason can know things-in-themselves and is capable of metaphysical knowledge. Understanding apprehends its objects by means of abstract concepts which are distinct from one another. For example, freedom and necessity indicate different aspects of experience and hence are capable of being combined by reason in a synthesis. Understanding is the faculty of abstraction which leads to contradictions. Reason is the faculty of synthesis by which contradictions are overcome. Logic culminates in the Absolute Idea, which is the unity of subject and object in self-consciousness. Thus, the Absolute Idea is for Hegel the logical expression for the Absolute Spirit.

The Absolute Spirit as the ultimate and unconditioned reality manifests itself in nature and the human spirit. This assertion points to Hegel's interpretation of religion. He conceived of religion as man's consciousness of God. It is the elevation of the human finite spirit to union with God the Infinite, Absolute Spirit.

For Hegel, the nature of religion is based upon his idealistic philosophy. Religion is identical with philosophy in its content, but different from it—only in its form. As the interest of philosophy is not merely theoretical knowledge of truth but knowledge of the Absolute Spirit which brings deliverance from the evils of finite existence, the interest of religion is not merely faith in the Absolute Spirit but knowledge of it as true. According to Hegel, religion is primarily a form of knowledge, although it also expresses itself in worship and conduct.

Hegel criticized theologians for advocating faith as independent of reason. He conceded that they are right in basing faith upon revelation in scripture. But he insisted that reason is required to interpret the meaning of revelation. Philosophical concepts are essential for the purpose of making revelation intelligible.

The Romantic view of religion represented by the early Schleiermacher was critically examined by Hegel. Feelings have their place in religion, but unexamined feeling is untrustworthy as a permanent element in religious experience. In fact, feeling by itself has a tendency to lead the self to subjectivity and away from God, the religious object.

The influence of Hegel upon religious thought was considerable. Theologians responded to his insights in both positive and negative ways. We will look at two responses to Hegel. Marxism is a response that has made an impact on secular and religious history. Kierkegaard's response has had a direct influence upon philosophy and theology.

Kierkegaard: Father of Existentialism[1]

The appearance of a figure so different from Hegel in the nineteenth century is important for understanding the dialectical character of Western thinking. The pendulum of ideas often swings from one extreme to another. The presence of Kierkegaard as a person and thinker illustrates this point.

Kierkegaard (1813–1855) was the founder and most brilliant spokesperson of a style of philsophizing known as existentialism. It would no doubt be a great disappointment to Kierkegaard to observe that his consciously unsystematic thought has become one more systematic statement of philosophy. But such is the case.

Søren Kierkegaard was born in 1813 to a father aged fifty-six and a mother aged forty-four. His early life and education were closely supervised by his father. His teacher demanded both the scholarly mastery of classical languages and an appreciation of literature. Through his stern father, Kierkegaard had laid upon him the guilt of an extreme pietistic Protestantism. Like Kant, Kierkegaard had a pietistic upbringing. But Kierkegaard's response was different. Kant retained a quiet inner confidence and peace. Kierkegaard was weighted down with guilt. In his youth, he reacted against the torment of his religious training through physical self-indulgence, eating, drinking and unusual dress. These distractions could not free him from the dark gloom which hung over him. He therefore decided to return to his life as a student and also became a pastor.

An important event in Kierkegaard's private life was his engagement to seventeen-year-old Regine Olson. He wrote compulsively of his feelings for Regine, of the philosophic significance of marriage, love and the problems of such commitment. But his breaking of the engagement together with the tone of his reflection indicate that the young woman was more a subject of meditation than a real live woman. Søren died at the early age of forty-two after writing a series of books on aesthetic, moral and religious topics.

The passionate center of Kierkegaard's thought and life was his confrontation with the ever-present terror of existential dread, the infinity of the universe and the meaninglessness of our brief life. This he saw as the human condition. He insists that this dread of death and meaninglessness must be faced and not shoved aside. At the same time, he found that this dread of death was heightened and complicated by the version of religion he inherited from his father. This was a brief background for a better appreciation of his brilliant reflection upon human existence.

For Kierkegaard, even the manner in which the free gift of God, eternal life, was presented was bad news—not good news. This message filled him with fear, dread, doubt, torment and a tortured self-examination. He was haunted by many questions and many doubts. Do I truly believe? Is my faith pure? Can I trust in the Lord? Am I worthy of God's grace? Kierkegaard writes out of the experience of an inner *hell*. His doubts and fears concerned his very *existence* as an individual, mortal creature longing to believe in God's promise in a personal manner. An abstract, impersonal, logical relationship of disembodied spirits was too often the manner in which theology had presented these matters. Kierkegaard stood before God as a person. He needed God's response to his inner torment.

In his struggle with the problem of faith, Kierkegaard tackled three opponents: 1. Established Christianity, the Lutheranism of nineteenth-century Denmark; 2. Bourgeois culture—the solid tradesman and lawyer types of his society; 3. Hegel, whose philosophy provided the ideological basis for culture in much of Europe.

Kierkegaard's three enemies were really one in different disguises. The Christianity of his day was bourgeois Christianity, buttressed and justified by the official philosophical system, Hegelism. The burghers were Establishment Christians who rationalized their beliefs through the use of Hegel. And Hegelianism was considered the purest product of reason. It assured that reign of the burghers (the middle class) and the ascendancy of their religion. In the language of H. Richard Niebuhr, the "Christ of Culture" reigned in Denmark.

Karl Marx, facing the same union of religion, philosophy and the ascendant bourgeoisie, turned his attack on the social and economic consequences. Marx was a secular man concerned with this-worldly issues of justice, poverty and work. Kierkegaard, by contrast, attacked on the religious front. He cared nothing for worldly happiness or misery. He insisted that the good Christians of

Denmark should begin to pay as much attention to eternal life as they paid to daily profit. We will look more carefully at Marx later. The side-by-side look at the two outlooks here may sharpen our appreciation for the contribution each was to make to theology in the twentieth century. In the case of existential as well as political and liberation theologies, there is a philosophical base. And one needs a serious engagement with philosophy in order to acquire a meaningful understanding of the resultant theologies.

There are two aspects of Kierkegaard's thought which claim our attention. These are the inwardness or subjectivity of truth, and the irrational "leap of faith." In some sense both of these perspectives are a negative response to Hegelianism. Hegel's thought was seen to be at once *rational* and *objective*.

In perspective, Hegel's philosophy was close to modern natural science. Knowledge was proclaimed as being objective, with no place for opinion or differences in personality. Hegelians saw themselves as rational discoverers of truth. Kierkegaard reversed this perspective by asserting that truth is subjectivity. According to Kierkegaard truth is inward, dependent upon the subject—it is personal. This is in conflict with the philosophical-scientific opinion of his day with its objective, impersonal assessment of truth.

Kierkegaard is not preoccupied with truth as conformity with the objective state of things in the world. He is concerned about salvation, according to the Christian message. Salvation is a matter in which the *how* of belief is important along with the *what* of belief. Hegel and his followers treated the Christian message as one small segment of a grand structure of objective knowledge.

Kierkegaard insisted that truth does not consist in the proper relationship between belief and the *object*. It lies in the proper relationship between belief and the *subject*—the individual who holds that belief. *How* one holds belief is the standard of its truth. In order for the belief to be true, it must be held passionately, unconditionally, absolutely, without inner reservation or doubt. Truth is manifest when one grasps it with the passion of inwardness.

The subjectivity of truth points directly to Kierkegaard's "leap of faith." Belief in God's promise of eternal life can have no rational justification, no evidence, no proof. All theistic proofs, from Aristotle to the present, are doomed to failure. According to Kierkegaard, there is no absolute gulf between the finite state of humanity and the infinite state of divinity, which renders all rational bridge-building futile. God can reach down to us, but how he does this is beyond our comprehension. Our approach to God by reason is aborted by its limits. Reason is therefore inadequate to the task of supporting our belief in the promises of God. Our hope is therefore absolutely irrational, a totally unjustifiable leap of faith. I must take the plunge and say, with all my heart, *credo*, I believe.

Even the titles of Kierkegaard's expositions of philosophical theology illustrate his rebellion of perspective over against Hegel. Recall the *Concluding Unscientific Postscript* and the *Philosophical Fragments*. Such words as "unscientific" and "fragments" are to be viewed in contrast to the scientific, rational and systematic thought represented by Hegel.

In *Philosophical Fragments*, Kierkegaard deals with the contrast between secular truth and religious truth, between subjective and objective thinking, between faith and reason, between wisdom and salvation. He contrasts Socrates, the greatest of all teachers, with Jesus the saviour. Secular knowledge of morality can be learned through rational self-reflection. Teachers like Socrates help us bring our moral knowledge to consciousness by probing questions that force us to justify our beliefs. Moral knowledge lies within: even a teacher like Socrates is only a helper. But salvation has to do with the fate of the soul. It is a matter of my existence, not merely my state of knowledge. Salvation cannot be acquired by one's own efforts. God must reach down and lift us up. The gulf between self and God must be crossed.

Jesus is God's instrument for bridging the gulf between God and humans. Jesus is Saviour. And since salvation concerns my *existence*, the actual historical reality of Jesus is all-important. It doesn't really matter whether Socrates ever lived. Once I have learned from the *Dialogues* of Plato how to engage in Socratic questioning, the historic Socrates no longer matters. But if the incarnation of God in Jesus Christ did not occur, if the cross is not a reality, then according to Kierkegaard there is no salvation. Salvation as a gift from God and eternal life are at stake. They have no rational ground—these are based upon an absolute leap of faith.

The thought of Kierkegaard is foundational to the influential existential movement of the twentieth century. Kierkegaard was a prophet without honor during his lifetime in his native land. A personal visit I made to Copenhagen to study Kierkegaard reveals that he is not popular there today. But one does not come to terms with existentialism in philosophy or theology without careful examination of the thought of this seminal thinker.

Marx and Dialectical Materialism

This is the place to consider the widespread influence of the thought of Karl Marx in the later nineteenth century and throughout the twentieth century. The thought of Marx has been behind many revolutions in recent years, as we well know. But it has also influenced theology in Latin America and political theology in Europe as well as theologies in most of the Third World. It is now being given careful consideration by some Afro-American theologians, e.g., Cornell West and to a lesser degree by James Cone. I, personally, have been challenged to seek a profounder knowledge of Marx and his movement. This is required if I am to be in conversation with my Black theologian colleagues as well as Third World theologians influenced by Marx and/or Marxism. No thorough or fair assessment of Marx's thought is possible without a careful study and analysis of it. The discussion here is limited to the core of Marx's philosophy and its implications for theology.

Karl Heinrich Marx was born in Trier, Germany, in 1818. Karl was the oldest son of a Jewish lawyer who was descended from a long line of rabbis. The young Marx was brought up as Protestant because his father became a Lutheran. The father shaped his son's intellectual outlook through his own rational and humanitarian outlook.

Karl was also influenced by Ludwig von Westphalen, a neighbor, Prussian government official and future father-in-law. Through Ludwig, Marx gained a life-long interest in Greek literature and philosophy, Dante and Shakespeare. After high school in Trier, Karl studied at the University of Bonn. He began the study of law in 1835 when he was only seventeen. He later transferred to the University of Berlin, where he gave up the study of law and turned to philosophy. At age twenty-three he received his doctorate from the University of Jena. His dissertation was entitled *On the Difference between the Democritean and Epicurean Philosophies of Nature*.

It was at Berlin that Karl Marx encountered the philosophy of Hegel, which was a dominant intellectual influence. Marx was deeply moved by Hegel's idealism and philosophy of history. He joined the young Hegelians, who saw in Hegel's philosophy the key to a new understanding of humankind, the world and history.

Whereas Marx was deeply influenced by Hegel's philosophy, he rejected or modified parts of it, especially upon his encounter with Feuerbach. Feuerbach questioned Hegel's idealism and substituted a philosophical materialism for it. Marx was greatly interested in human thought and behavior. Whereas Hegel saw the thought and behavior of a particular epoch as the working in all humans of an identical spirit, Feuerbach contended that the generating influence of our thoughts was the total sum of the material circumstances of any historic period.

In Feuerbach's *Essence of Christianity*, Marx observed an "inversion" of Hegel's assumption that Spirit or Idea is primary. Feuerbach argued, instead, for the primacy of the material order. Human beings and not God are the basic reality. God is the product of human thought and not the other way around. This inversion of Hegel's idealism and the resulting materialism inspired Marx and provided him with one of the most decisive and characteristic elements in his philosophy.

His experiences as a journalist in Paris and Brussels, his study of the French Revolution and his experience with workers, are among the vital influences upon his outlook. After being expelled from Paris a second time, Marx moved to London, where he was to spend the remainder of his life. During his first stay in Paris, Marx met Friedrich Engels, son of a German textile manufacturer, who was to be a lifetime associate.

Marx wrote his famous *Capital* while in London. He did so amidst incredible poverty and personal illness. He experienced the loss of two children, as well as his wife, before his own death of pleurisy at the age of sixty-five. His plight was serious and his family suffered much. His writings gave him some relief, as did some financial assistance from Engels. It is odd that Marx spent so much time in seclusion and study, especially in the British Museum. He did not involve himself in revolutionary activities—i.e. organizing workers among the masses who were subject to the evil of the Industrial Revolution. It would appear that his ideology, rather than his personal example, was to prevail.

In a real sense, then, Marx provides a philosophy for action and change. His comments on Feuerbach are instructive. He indicates that in the past, philosophers have *interpreted* the world differently. The point now is to *change* it. He grounded his major insights in Hegel's dialectical view of history and Feuerbach's emphasis on the primacy of the material order. He sought to provide a program of forging these insights into a full-scale instrument of social analysis. The goal was to provide a vigorous and practical program of action.

The core of Marxist thought consists in the analysis of three basic elements: 1. the major epochs of history, 2. the causal power of the material order, and 3. the source and role of ideas. This analysis was meant to uncover what each of these elements means and show how they are related to each other.

While Marx was in Brussels, he helped organize a German Worker's Union. In 1847, at a meeting in London, this group united with several other groups in Europe. Engels became the first secretary. Marx was asked to draft a statement of principles. This statement appeared in 1848 as *The Manifesto of the Communist Party*. Already in this document, Marx had formulated his basic doctrine. He attempted to establish certain principles as follows: 1. that the existence of classes is only bound up with particular historic phases in the development of production; 2. that the class struggle necessarily leads to the dictatorship of the proletariat; 3. that the dictatorship itself only constitutes the transition to the abolition of all classes and to a classless society. While in London, in *Capital* Marx built on the foundation laid in the *Manifesto*. In the preface to the latter work, he states that its ultimate aim is to lay bare the economic law of motion of modern society. This law of motion became his theory of dialectical materialism.

We shall now discuss the *five epochs: change, determinism, history*, the *material order* and *ideas*. A brief critique will follow.

Marx indicated that the class struggle is bound up with particular historic phases. He divided history into five separate epochs as follows: 1. the primitive communal, 2. slave, 3. feudal, 4. capitalist, and 5. the socialist and communist phases. What Marx sought through this division of history was the "law of motion" which would explain the reason why these particular epochs unfolded as they did. This would not only enable him to understand the past, but would help to predict the future. He assumed that the behavior of individuals and societies is subject to the same kind of analysis as are the objects of physical and biological science.

He considered the commodity and value products of economics as being of the same order as those minute elements dealt with in microscopic anatomy. When he analyzed the structure of each epoch, he either imposed upon it or abstracted from it the fact of class conflict as the decisive force at work.

Here Marx relied heavily upon the Hegelian concept of *dialectic* to explain it. While rejecting Hegel's idealism, he accepted the general theory of the dialectic movement of history, which I review briefly here. Hegel had argued that ideas develop in a dialectic way, through the action and reaction of thought, describing this dialectic from *thesis* to *antithesis* and then to *synthesis*, where the synthesis becomes a new thesis and so on. In addition, Hegel saw the external world (social, political and economic) as the embodiment of ideas. Thus, the development of the external world stems from the prior development of ideas. While accepting this thought-structure, Marx pours a different meaning into the receptacle—moving from idealism to materialism. He assumed an opposite interpretation from Hegel's intention.

According to Marx, *change* is necessary and inevitable. History shows that social and economic orders are in a process of change. The material order is all that there is, and all is in a ceaseless state of change. Change, however, is not identical to growth. Change means the emergence of new structures, novel forms. But quantitative change leads to that which is qualitatively new. For instance, as one increases the temperature of water, it becomes warmer, but it finally reaches the point where it turns to vapor. If the process is reversed, it changes from a liquid to a solid state, to ice. For Marx, this is an analogy of the way change is manifested in history. Quantitative change in the economic order finally forces a qualitative change in the arrangements of society. Thus society has moved from the *primitive communal* to the *slave*, and in turn to the *feudal* and *capitalist* epochs. As the role of the working class increases in a capitalist society, production is centralized, labor is socialized, and eventually change is incompatible with the nature of capitalism. There occurs a *quantitative leap* to a new order. In this way quantity is transformed into quality.

History is determined by inexorable law. Marx perceived a fundamental contradiction in the nature of things causing the dialectic movement. There is no way to prevent the ultimate unfolding of the essence of things. All things are related to each other *causally*. There are no isolated events in physical nature or human behavior in history. There is a definite and inexorable process in history as in nature. Marx did not apply a mechanical determinism to history. In fact, he did not apply it to the individual. But he did insist that there is an inner logic in events which causes history to move from one epoch to the next with a relentless determinism. On the basis of this, he predicted that capitalism would fall and the qualitatively different social order or socialism and communism would develop.

The end of history, according to Marx, would be socialism and finally communism. Here, again, Marx followed Hegel's theory in an inverted way. For Hegel, the dialectic process comes to an end when the Idea of freedom is perfectly realized, for by definition this would mean the end of all conflict and struggle. Marx, on the other hand, conceived of the dialectic of opposites in the material order — i.e., in the struggle between classes. He insists that when the inner contradictions between the classes are finally resolved, the principal cause of change will disappear. A classless society will emerge, and balance and equilibrium will be perpetual. No further development of history will take place. There will be nothing to provide conflict or impel history to any future epoch.

It is to be understood that Marx's theory rested upon a distinction between the order of material reality and human thought. This led him to make a distinction between the *substructure* and the *superstructure* of society. The *substructure* is the material order, which contains the force which energizes or moves history. The *superstructure*, on the other hand, consists in human ideas which reflect the configurations of the material order.

According to Marx, *materialism* is the sum-total of the natural environment. This includes all of inorganic nature, the organic world, social life, and human consciousness. Democritus defined matter as atoms or irreducible tiny particles, but Marx saw it as objective reality which exists outside the human mind. Again, Democritus considered his atoms to be the bricks of the universe. Marx was not concerned about a single form of matter in all things. He recognized great diversity in the material world and did not reduce everything to one form of matter. The material world, then, contains everything in the natural order that exists outside the human mind. Marx does not see a place for a spiritual reality (i.e., God) that exists outside the human mind as something other than nature.

The assertion that human beings possess minds means only that organic matter has developed to the point where the cerebral cortex leads to thought. The human mind, at the same time, has been conditioned by the labor of humans as social beings. Marx exalts the primacy of the material order. Mental activity is a secondary by-product of matter. The transformation from animal to human came as humans acquired the ability to use tools to control such forces as fire, which increased the variety of food and aided the further development of the brain. Thus the material reality is basic. The mental realm is derived from it.

In a further understanding of the material order, Marx discusses the *factors* and *relations* of production. In order to live, humans must secure food, clothing, and shelter. In order to have these, humans must produce. Wherever we find human beings, factors of production are present: raw materials, instruments, experienced labor skill and other means whereby things are produced to sustain life. This points directly to the relations of production, which was Marx's greater concern.

Marx was preoccupied with production as a social act. Humans struggle, according to Marx, against nature as well as utilize nature as groups or as societies. Marx's statement of the relations of production is the core of his social analysis. The key to the relations of production center upon property. Those who own the means of production dominate the social order. Those who labor, but do not share in ownership of the means of production or the fruits of production (i.e., slave or hired), are exploited. The ownership of property divides society between those who have and those who have not. This is true of all the epochs of history leading up to capitalism. In capitalism also, workers who do not own the means of production sell their labor to the capitalist in order to survive.

Although in all periods there is a conflict between classes, it is particularly violent under capitalism. There are at least three characteristics of the class struggle under capitalism. First, the classes are now reduced basically to two: the owners, or bourgeoisie, and the workers, or proletariat. Secondly, the relations of those classes to each other rests upon a contradiction. Both participate in production, but the mode of distribution of what is produced is to the disadvantage of the worker. The price of labour is determined by supply and demand. The large supply of workers tends to lower wages down to a subsistence level. At the same time, the products produced can be sold for more than it costs to hire the labor. Marx's analysis is based upon the labor theory of value, that the value of the product is created by the amount of labor required to produce it. Since the product of labor can be sold for more than the cost of labor, the capitalist reaps the difference. This he designates as *surplus value*. The existence of surplus value is the contradiction in the capitalist system. Exploitation is inherent in capitalism because of the manner in which wages operate. Marx saw this development in capitalism as based upon scientific reasons stated in his interpretation of history. But he insisted that the class conflict caused by the contradiction of surplus value would force the dialectic to the next stage of history.

The third characteristic of this class struggle follows. Marx predicted that the condition of workers in capitalism would become progressively worse. The poor would become poorer and more numerous. The rich would become richer and fewer. The masses would eventually take over all the means of production. Marx saw this result as inevitable. As long as the means of production remained in the hands of a few, the class struggle would continue. But the dialectical process would manifest itself in socialism or communism, resolving the contradiction and ending the dialectic of history. Because of the conflictual nature of history, wars, violence and revolutions are possible, even probable. The function of the revolutionary activities of the working class is to speed up a determined and inevitable happening.

Finally, we take a brief look at the origin and role of *ideas*. According to Marx, each epoch has its own ideas. Ideas are formulated in the areas of religion, morality and law. Hegel argued that humans agreed for the most part in their religious moral and juristic thought because there was a universal Spirit, the Idea, in them. Marx, on the contrary, insisted that the ideas of each epoch grow out of and reflect the material conditions of the historic period. Thinking comes after the material order has affected the human mind. According to Marx, there is a relationship between human consciousness and the material environment. The consciousness of humans, however, does not determine their being. On the contrary, the social being of humans determines their consciousness.

According to Marx, the source of ideas is rooted in the material order. Such ideas as justice, goodness and even salvation are only various ways of rationalizing the existing order. Justice, for example, represents the will of the economically dominant class to maintain the *status quo*. Justice, then, is understood in relative terms. Marx rejected the notion of a universal and eternal norm of justice. Each epoch will have its own set of ideas; for ideas reflect the inner order of the relations of production.

The conflict of ideas within a society arises from the dynamic nature of the economic order. The dialectical process has its material aspect and also its ideological side. Members of society are related to the dialectical process by belonging to different classes. Their interests are different, and for this reason their ideas are opposed. As the order of the economic situation changes, ideas must change if they are to retain the substance of reality. According to Marx, an astute observer can discover the direction in which history is moving and adjust thinking and behavior to it.

The dialectical process involves the passing of some things and the emergence of new things. One epoch dies and another is born, and the process is continuous. Thus, those who assume the objective reality of eternal principles of such things as justice, goodness and righteousness are off-base. Such notions, according to Marx, do not refer to reality itself, since the material order is the only reality and it is constantly changing. Productive relations constitute the structure of society. Here is the real foundation on which legal and political superstructures rest. Production determines the character of the social, political and spiritual processes of life.

Marx was impatient with do-gooders, reformers and others who espouse ideas which bear no relationship to the economic reality. Ideas, according to him, are chiefly a reflection of the material order. Beyond this, they have a limited role. Ideas, for instance, cannot determine the direction of history. They can only hinder or accelerate the inexorable dialectic. Marx did not morally condemn capitalism. According to his philosophy, capitalism is caused by the "law of motion of society." Marx believed that his analysis was that of a scientist. He described through his thought what for him was objective reality. Thus he presents what in the history of Western thought is designated dialectical materialism.

The ideas and the project of Marx have had widespread consequences in shaping the geo-political realities of this century. These consequences are too numerous and too well-known to claim our attention here. We are moved, rather, by the impact which Marx and Marxism has had upon developing theologies in Latin America, Europe, Africa and Asia. Whereas for Marx ideas had secondary importance, both the ideological and the socio-politico-economic influence of his contributions have in many ways dominated the twentieth century. No one can be theologically literate today while ignoring the influence of Marx and Marxism.

The Legacy of Hegel, Kierkegaard and Marx

I claim only a limited scope for this volume. In this vein, I have selected three representative philosophers from the nineteenth century: Hegel, Kierkegaard and Marx. Hegel's influence appears to be seminal and powerful; he was the original creative genius.

Both Kierkegaard and Marx receive important insights from Hegel which set the stage for their own important reflections. Hegel proposed to gather up all time and all existence, and in his rational system treated nature and God, Spirit and Idea all together. Kierkegaard reacted negatively to Hegel's system and the logic upon which is stood. This led him to put all of his genius in the service of faith and individual persons. Marx takes Hegel's dialectic of logic and history seriously. But through insights from Feuerbach into the ultimacy of the human and his own materialism, he inverted the Hegelian idealism into a dialectical materialism, which we have already described. Hegel, Kierkegaard and Marx, among others, have influenced the ideology, philosophy and theology of the twentieth century. We still do our reflection by the light which they have cast upon our pathway.

XI

Contemporary Religious Thought (II): Focus on the Twentieth Century

The Context: Persons and Movements

The year 1914 brought to an end the optimism of the nineteenth century. During the next four years, thirty nations, representing 1.4 billion people on six continents, were at war. This was the most devastating conflict that humankind had ever seen. Science and technology, which symbolized inevitable progress, was now being used for mass destruction. The toll in the killing and maiming of human beings tells the tragic story. By the 1918 armistice, some ten million combatants were dead and twenty million were wounded. About ten million civilians were either killed, or lost to disease and famine. The destruction of property and non-human life was awesome.

The Situation

After a brief decade of economic recovery, we were stunned again. The United States fell into an economic depression with the collapse of the stock market in 1929. In the next few years, the depression spread to other industrialized nations in Europe. Factories shut down, banks were closed and unemployment soared. There followed much anxiety, hopelessness and despair.

In the aftermath of war and depression, totalitarianism arose, regimenting people and suppressing their individuality. All this was motivated by national dreams of conquest and expansion. World War II was to follow by the late 1930s. This proved to be an even more devastating war than World War I. The whole world was involved. Seventy million people fought and thirty million died, civilians as well as soldiers. The Holocaust took place during that war. Nazi leaders sought systematically to exterminate Europe's Jewish population. Some six million Jews were eliminated. This terrible war closed with the innovation of an even more ominous era—the atomic age. On August 6, 1945, an atomic bomb was dropped on Hiroshima, Japan. This bomb, prepared by U.S. and European scientists, was 2,000 times more powerful than any previous bomb. It destroyed most of the city, killed 68,000 people and left a radioactive atmosphere that injured thousands more.

There is much more we could say about the twentieth century from the point of view of minorities in the West as well as from the outlook of Third World peoples. For instance, America (U.S.) experienced a Civil War in the 1860s which led to the freeing of black slaves. The history of these freed slaves for the next hundred or so years has helped shape their interpretation of history. The late and mid-twentieth century has marked the demise of colonialism, independence and nation-building in most of the Third World. Through rapid travel, telecommunication and commerce, the world has become a global village. Philosophy can no longer ignore these realities. Thus what we do here is limited by the focus selected for this volume.

For reasons of delimitation, this final chapter will emphasize Anglo-American initiatives in philosophy. We will be concerned with those thought-movements that have had significant influence upon religious thought in general and theology in particular: pragmatism, personalism, process and analytic philosophies. In each case I shall introduce a seminal thinker and then discuss the movement before indicating how it influenced theology. Where it seems appropriate, I will make a brief reference to more than one thinker and show how each contributed to the development of a particular thought-movement.

Pragmatism

One of the greatest of American pragmatists was William James (1842–1910). He excelled in both psychology and philosophy. We are here concerned primarily with his philosophy and its contribution to religious knowledge.

James's philosophy of pragmatism (truth is workability) brought into focus an aspect of Kant's earlier synthesis—viz. the importance of practical reason. He emphasized the freedom of the human will and declared that truth was judged by its practical consequences. An idea was true if it made a difference in the world.

James graduated from the Harvard Medical School in 1870. He soon taught anatomy and psychology, and by 1879 was lecturing in philosophy. This progression was natural for James. He always probed scientific questions for the more general, philosophical considerations behind them.

In psychology and philosophy, James was self-taught. His wealthy father reacted against rigid indoctrination of his children in religion and education. He wanted them to be capable of independent thinking, and for this purpose moved them from one school to another. William James established himself as an original mind in *Principles of Psychology* (1890). Later he studied religious phenomena and philosophy and made original contributions in *Varieties of Religious Experience* and *Pragmatism*. He captured the optimism of his day—the spirit of a young nation, caught in the promise of progress. He emphasized "possibility thinking"—the "will-to-believe."

James states his case as follows: "What you want is a philosophy that will not only exercise your powers of intellectual abstraction, but that will make some positive connection with this actual world of finite human lives."[1]

Paul Tillich provides an apt summary statement of James' pragmatism:

Pragmatism, as developed by William James . . . reveals the philosophical motive behind this elevation of experience to the highest ontological rank, viz. reality is identified with experience. The motive is to deny the split between an ontological subject and ontological objects, for, once established, this split cannot be overcome, the possibility of knowledge cannot be explained and the unity of life and its processes remains a mystery.[2]

This existential reaction took many forms of expression. Its impact was deeply felt across Europe, but it also found philosophical and theological expression in the United States. It was in the U.S. that John Macquarrie (Scottish) and Paul Tillich (German) gave classic expression to theological existentialism.

Depth Psychology

We would be remiss not to mention the impact of the thought of Sigmund Freud (1856–1939), an Austrian neurologist who founded psychoanalysis. The thought of Freud is especially important to existentialism as well as to the theological treatment of anxiety. A succinct look at his contribution is important here.

Freud made the tripartite division of the psyche into *id, ego* and *superego*. The *id* derives from the needs of our biological nature striving for satisfaction, in a completely uncoordinated and uncircumspect way. It consists of unconscious impulses.

The *ego* tries to coordinate the drives which constitute the *id*. The *ego* replaces "the pleasure principle" by the "reality principle." It takes into account the conditions imposed by the external world. It is the relationship between the *ego* and the *id*, rather than those parts of the psyche which are conscious and unconscious, which is of primary importance to psychoanalysis.

The *superego* is roughly equivalent to conscience. It often treats the *ego* harshly, particularly in neurotic states. It is important that the *ego* be on good terms with the *superego* and that it should be in control of the *id*.

According to Freud, *anxiety* is the ego's admission of its weaknesses. Three kinds of anxiety may be distinguished: *realistic* anxiety in relation to the external world, *moral* anxiety in relation to the *superego*, and *neurotic* anxiety in relation to the impulses of the *id*. The *ego* exercises influence over the *id* by putting into operation the pleasure-unpleasure principle. This principle influences the *id* through the medium of anxiety. It is thus that impulses are repressed.

In Socrates, injunction "know thyself" we see the basis of Freud's project. Freud emphasizes that there is great danger in one's refusal to be conscious of one's disagreeable emotions. The failure of consciousness may lead to uncontrollable behavior. Increase in awareness may lead to greater freedom of action.

Freud pays a lot of attention to two instincts: hunger and sex. For him, both are complex and comprehensive instincts. He denies that his outlook depends upon any philosophical or religious wisdom, however ancient. He insists that his view is independent and scientific.

Regardless of Freud's intentions or claims, his views have had a wide influence upon religious thought everywhere. This is especially true of the theological community in the United States. Tillich drew heavily upon depth psychology as well as existentialism in his system of philosophical theology. The theological and philosophical reaction to Freud has been positive and negative.[3]

In my judgment, James is most representative of the American philosophical and religious outlook. It is for this reason that his thought has had such a wide influence ever since his own time. He has had a wide influence upon religious thought, both philosophical and theological.

The Existential Reaction

I would be remiss not to mention the impact of existentialism upon the twentieth century. It paralleled the earlier work of Kierkegaard, but it was especially focused upon the despair of a world in which all traditional cultural values seem to have collapsed.

Jean-Paul Sartre (1905–1980) had worked in the French underground movement resisting Nazism. He spoke for a generation that believed that it had to order its own world and create its own values. A human being just existed and had to create its own values. A human being just existed and had to create its own essence. Thus human beings were "condemned" to be free. Sartre rejected God and anything that seemed to limit human freedom. He proclaimed that "hell is other people," and conceived of death as the final absurdity of existence.

Whitehead and the Philosophy of Process

Alfred North Whitehead was born in 1861. He lived until 1947. It is important that he never lost his belief in progress, considering the good and bad experiences of the history of his long life. He also lived on both sides of the Atlantic, in England and the United States.

Whitehead's early training was in the British preparatory school tradition of the Latin and Greek classics. After studying at Cambridge, he taught mathematics there for twenty-five years. At fifty, he moved to London, where he studied and taught the philosophy of science until his retirement at sixty-two. He was then invited to teach philosophy at Harvard, although he had never formally studied or taught philosophy. It was during his next thirteen years that Whitehead did most of his creative writing.

Whitehead brought classical philosophy and contemporary science together in his reflection. He agreed with the Greek classicists that there was a real world in which everything was inter-related and that the human task was to understand it. But in his view the answers which the Greeks had given in metaphysics and epistemology were no longer adequate.

Modern science had changed the focus of philosophy, Whitehead asserted. Reality was not now understood in terms of substances and essences, but in terms of processes and relationships. Physicists do not need to define what an atom is; they only need to understand how it acts. Psychologists no longer ask the question, "What is a human?" The issues now are, "How do humans behave?", "How can they adjust to their environment?" Whitehead's philosophy took these changes of focus into account.

Whitehead was involved in both natural science and philosophy. In addition, he was a religious person who reflected upon it from the inside of belief. Religion, however, is individual rather than institutional. He was also of the "once-born" type rather than among the "twice-born."

Whitehead was aware that modern science provides a climate quite different from the world of medieval religious thinkers. The medieval thinkers believed in the purpose and rationality of God. The personal energy of Jehovah was combined with the reason of the Greek philosophers. We have now entered into a climate of "scientific materialism." This outlook presupposes the ultimate fact of an irreducible brute matter. This material, spread throughout space in a flux of configurations, is believed to be senseless, purposeless and valueless. All is governed by mechanical law or external relations, which do not spring from the nature of its being.

Whitehead rejects this scientific materialism. It is based upon the fallacy of "misplaced concreteness" or the error of mistaking the abstract for the concrete. It is in the nature of science to be limited in its focus on one aspect of the world. Philosophy, on the other hand, is not thus limited and can seek an understanding of the whole. Philosophy harmonizes the sciences by pointing to the relationship of one science to others. It also completes the outreach of the sciences by comparing them with other concrete experiences — e.g., those expressed through art, poetry and religion.

Whitehead's philosophy is rightly called the philosophy of organism. Material and mental substances are highly complex "societies" or entities which are organic in nature. Reality as a whole is composed of organisms rather than material atoms. Whitehead, therefore, rejects a materialistic interpretation of the theory of evolution. The theory of evolution has often received a one-dimensional interpretation. It has been discussed in reference to adaptation to the environment, the struggle for existence, and natural selection. But, according to Whitehead, there is another side, usually neglected. This is creativeness, the capacity of societies of cooperating organisms to create their own environment. Evolution is characterized by "friendly help" as well as "the struggle for existence." The concept of organisms is not confined to the biological realm; it is likewise extended to the physical realm—there is no discontinuity between the two realms.

George F. Thomas has captured this point of view from Whitehead in the following words:

> This interrelatedness of all things in space and time is made possible by the "prehension" or "apprehension" by each of all the others, so that a natural entity is a gathering together of things into the unity of a prehension. A concrete fact or actual entity is a "process," and nature is a "structure of evolving processes."[4]

Religion is for Whitehead the art or theory of the internal life. It depends upon the person as well as the nature of things. Whitehead's interest in religion centers upon its power to transform individual lives. In his view, the higher religions are concerned at once with the value of an individual for itself and the values of the objective world. "World-loyalty" is the merger of the individual claim with the universal demand. Thus, according to Whitehead, religion is what the individual does with one's own solitariness together with world-loyalty.

Religion is concerned with permanence and change. It is the vision of something which stands beyond, behind and within the passing flux of immediate things. It is real, but also waiting to be realized. It is at once an ultimate ideal and a hopeless quest. Permanence can be snatched only out of flux, and the passing moment can find its proper intensity only as it submits to permanence. Religion, therefore, seeks the realization of value in the midst of time and the conservation of value after it is realized. God's purpose is the attainment of value in time. God, according to Whitehead, is an eternal principle of order who transcends the flux of events. God provides the final cause which guides every creature in the process of attaining new value.

Whitehead's understanding of religion is reasonable. It is essential that religion be not divorced from reason and allowed to become a matter of blind emotion. Religious experience and belief must be accompanied by emotion if they are to have transforming power in life, but they must be expressed in terms which are compatible with scientific knowledge.

As we turn to Whitehead's metaphysics, we are aware of Platonic and Christian influences. His thought is not traditional—he uses all ideas according to his own philosophic and religious vision. He combines the empiricists' demand for knowledge based upon experience with the rationalists' belief in the ultimate rationality and coherence of all reality. His thought starts from observation of the facts of experience, includes imaginative generalizations, but concludes with a renewed observation of facts. One finds there descriptive generalizations and conclusions that are tentative rather than final. He is not limited to the Cartesian requirement of clear and distinct ideas. He also pays attention to vague experiences on the fringes of consciousness.

According to Whitehead, the world consists of a plurality of "actual entities." An actual entity is not a substance, but "a process"—whose being is constituted by its becoming. It is an individual unit of becoming which completes itself and is succeeded by other such units. All actual entities are individual manifestations of a generic activity called "creativity." Creativity is not itself an actual entity; it is the creative activity expressed by all actual entities. In sum, an actual entity is a process, an instance of the creativity of the world which perpetually brings forth novelty.

The world consists of a plurality of actual entities. Each is a process of becoming through the integration of data into a novel unity of feeling. Each actual entity receives its data through physical feelings of past actual entities and conceptual feelings of eternal objects or forms of definiteness. These feelings are integrated under the guidance of a subjective aim in a process which culminates in satisfaction. When an actual entity perishes, it attains objective immortality as a potential datum or object for succeeding actual entities. The aim of every actual entity is intensity of feeling and thus the realization of value. This requires order based upon the dominance of common characteristics in enduring societies of actual entities. Such societies require a favorable wider social environment with natural laws which are neither necessary nor immutable.[5]

Whitehead stands at the fountainhead of a movement known as "process" thought. It is manifest in theology as well as philosophy. Such diverse thinkers as Charles Hartshorne, John B. Cobb, Nelson Wieman and Teilhard de Chardin are representative.[6] Here we have been concerned mainly about the core of Whitehead's theory of knowledge. But his metaphysics, like that of Aristotle, leads directly to a form of teleological pantheism.

Personalism

Personalism does not receive the attention it deserves in the treatment of American religious thought. As one trained in British neoliberal theology under such persons as John Baillie at Edinburgh and Herbert Farmer at Cambridge, I was soon struck by the emphasis upon common themes with the Boston School of Personalism. I had an immediate engagement, of an intellectual nature, with Edgar Brightman and Albert Knudson. But it was the influence of Harold DeWolf, who was at Wesley while I taught at Howard, that had a great personal impact upon me during my formative years. My admiration for the thought of M. L. King, Jr., together with DeWolf's direct influence upon him during his student years, has reinforced my sense of the importance of personalism.

Personalism is a philosophical perspective for which "person" is the ontological ultimate and for which personality is the fundamental explanatory principle of reality. It is mainly a twentieth-century movement, with historical antecedents (with idealism) which are similar but not strictly personalist. I have just mentioned some encounters with British thinkers with similar ideas. But though there are advocates of personalism in many parts of the world, my concern will be mainly within the United States.

The term "person" comes from the Latin *persona*, meaning mask and/or actor. It came to refer to a role and to human dignity in relation to others. This usage is strengthened by theological language, for which *persona* is the Latin equivalent of the Greek *hypostasis* (standing under). Both terms are closely related to the Greek *ousia* (substance). These associations foreshadow the fact that personalism attaches to personality, both in value (dignity) and in being (person as a substance). Personalists have attached more significance to the definition of Boethius, who asserted that a person is an individual substance of a rational nature (*persona est naturae rationabilis individua substantia*).[7]

Personalism is usually theistic. The personalism of J. M. E. McTaggart is atheistic and considered an exception. Again, personalism is generally influenced by Greek metaphysical motifs and motifs from biblical religion. Nevertheless, it considers itself a system defensible on philosophical grounds and is not dependent upon merely theological affirmations.

Descartes, Leibniz, Berkeley, Hegel and Lotze are among those who have contributed to the personalist outlook. Descartes, for example, posited the primacy of personal experience and identified it with mental substance. This Cartesian principle asserts itself in Brightman, who observes:

> A person is a complex unity of consciousness, which identifies itself with its past self in memory, determines itself by its freedom, is purposive and value-seeking, private yet communicating, and potentially rational.[8]

Personalism expresses itself in several forms—both realistic and idealistic. I use the term here to designate "personal idealism." It is idealistic: all reality is personal. It is pluralistic: reality is a society of persons. It is theistic: God is the ultimate person and, as such, is the grounds of all being and the creator of finite persons.

The thought of Bowne (1847–1910) is foundational for the Boston School of Personalism. Bowne was influenced by Berkeley, Kant and Lotze. He was a pluralistic idealist who was explicitly theistic. The Divine Person is not only the creator of finite selves or persons, but is also the World Ground. God's self-directing and intelligent agency shows itself in the order and continuity of the phenomenal world. Bowne on the one hand opposed Hegelian absolutism and Spencerian evolutionism, and on the other opposed fundamentalism and dogmatic supernaturalism.

Albert C. Knudson (1873–1953) and Edgar Sheffield Brightman (1874–1953) were Bowne's students. Knudson was a theologian and Brightman was a philosopher. Both taught at Boston University. Brightman is generally considered as the most important among Bowne's Boston students. He taught at Boston from 1919 until his death. Brightman, a creative and original thinker, developed a comprehensive personalistic system.

Brightman posited an epistemological dualism of what he called "the shining present" (the situation-experienced) and "the illuminating absent" (the situation-believed-in). Immediate experience is the inescapable starting point, but experience always refers beyond itself (self-transcendence). The possibility of reference is found in the activity of the mind in knowing. The adequacy of reference is determined by the criterion of coherence. Maximum coherence in interpreting experience is maximum truth. In his emphasis on the tentativeness and testing of hypothesis, Brightman is empirical. In his emphasis on system and inclusive order, he is rationalistic.

In his metaphysics, Brightman maintained that everything that exists (or subsists) is in, of, or for a mind on some level. He defined personalism as the hypothesis that all being is a personal experient (a complex unity of consciousness) or some phase or aspect of one or more such experients. The natural world is understood as an order within or as a function of the mind of God. Finite persons are created by the uncreated Person. Human persons are therefore centers of intrinsic value. Again, the value dimension of human experience provides the evidence of a religious dimension of reality. Hence, God is the source and conserver of values.

The most distinctive, and in some ways the most controversial, aspect of Brightman's thought is his revision of the traditional idea of God. Brightman argued that if we are to take personality seriously as a basic explanatory model, then we must accept a temporalist view of God. If God is personal, he is omni-temporal, not timeless. He also insisted that the view that God is omnipotent could not be maintained without seriously qualifying the divine goodness. Evil, suffering and death makes this so. In the face of evil, Brightman concludes that the will of God is limited by non-rational conditions (the Given) within the divine nature that are neither created nor approved by the divine will. God maintains constant and growing (but never complete) control of the Given. For Brightman, God is infinite in goodness, but finite in power. This means that Brightman's views were seriously questioned and opposed by theological colleagues, even at Boston, like Knudson and DeWolf.[9]

Boston Personalism has contributed decisively to liberalizing the leadership of the Methodist church. Due to the fact that many black scholars studied at Boston (from many denominations) for advanced degrees, Boston Personalism has been greatly manifest in black churches. M. L. King, Jr. (a Baptist) is one sterling example. King, however, accepted Personalism as interpreted by his mentor, DeWolf. But as he discusses some moral issues, it is clear that Brightman had directly influenced him. The pervasive impact of Boston Personalism upon the American theological, ecclesiological and philosophical population is widespread. And, as we have observed, it is by no means restricted to those associated with the Boston School of Theology.

Language Analysis and Religious Belief

Analytical philosophy is a well-known philosophic activity in the contemporary English-speaking world.[10] It is more like a *movement* than a *school* because if its variety, but it has certain clear distinguishing characteristics. It seems strange that the person who gave the greatest thrust to the movement came from Austria-Hungary rather than from Britain. Ludwig Wittgenstein was born in 1889 in Austria-Hungary. Karl, his father, was a stern, unbending man. He was a millionaire in the steel industry. Karl loved music. Johannes Brahms was a frequent guest in his home.

Karl insisted that his sons follow him in business. Of five sons, the two oldest desired to pursue a career in music. The oldest committed suicide after his father denied him the opportunity. A second son met the same fate.

In 1913, Karl died. A third son took his own life in World War I, rather than be captured. A fourth son, Paul, became a successful concert pianist.

The woman in the family were gifted and strong-willed. Ludwig's mother, Leopoldine, was an outstanding pianist. His oldest sister, Hermine, was an excellent painter. His youngest sister, Margaretta, was the rebel of the family. She was a close friend of Sigmund Freud. She helped him escape from Austria when Hitler took over.

These talents and conflicts in the family influenced Ludwig. His father believed in private tutoring in the home. Ludwig was fourteen before he had the opportunity for much study away from home. He first studied engineering. He went to Linz Realschule, where Hitler had studied. He soon discovered that he was more interested in philosophy and ethics. Though he did not have classical training in philosophy, he soon became excited over Kierkegaard. Like the famous Dane, cultural as well as personal problems were to occupy him for the remainder of his life.

After Linz, he studied at Berlin. In 1908, he went to the University of Manchester, where he studied aerodynamics. He then became interested in mathematics, and in 1911 went to Cambridge to study under Bertrand Russell. It was while studying with Russell that he was sure that he should become a philosopher.

After two years at Cambridge, Ludwig retreated to a remote section of Norway, where he remained until the outbreak of World War I in 1914. He then enlisted as a volunteer in the Austrian artillery. While serving on the Eastern front, he compiled a notebook on philosophical issues. These notes became the basis for his *Tractatus Logico-Philosophicus*. Upon being captured by the Italians in 1917, he completed this work in prison. A copy was sent to Russell, who endorsed the work with great affirmation. The

Tractatus was published in 1921. With it Wittgenstein sparked a revolution in philosophical reflection.

According to the *Tractatus*, philosophy is an activity rather than a set of theories. Most of the problems of philosophy stem from a misuse of language. Philosophy provides no pictures of reality and can neither confirm nor refute scientific investigation. Its fundamental task is to teach us the logical form of propositions. Philosophy is a battle against the bewitchment of our intelligence by means of language.

The greater part of the *Tractatus* is devoted to language, its nature and relation to the world. The author presents this relationship in terms of "a picture theory of meaning." Language consists of statements or propositions that picture the world. Just as a picture has something in common with that which is pictured, language has a logical form in common with the world it pictures. This logical form is observed by ordinary language. The task of philosophy is to clear up this obscure language and ultimately develop a language that will more perfectly picture the world.

This clearing up of ordinary language is to be done by analysis. Propositions are made up of names (which stand for objects) and a logical form. These names and their logical form create a picture. This picture is the meaning of the proposition. The role of analysis is to find these names and clearly show the logical form. For example, let us analyze the proposition: "John is going to the store." We discover the objects the names "John" and "store" stand for and then we clearly show the logical form of the statement: "John is going to the store."

The study of this use of language through the method of analysis led Wittgenstein to distinguish between *factual* language and *religious* and *ethical* language. Factual propositions are those that could be analyzed. They refer to a state of affairs in the world. According to this outlook, terms such as God or Being are not really names, they do not point to anything. According to Wittgenstein, God does not reveal himself *in* the world. In like manner, ethical assertions cannot be analyzed. The nature of the Good has nothing to do with facts and cannot be explained by propositions.

Wittgenstein's intentions were not necessarily negative, but fundamental to his project. He lived in a situation where values were under constant attack. He therefore sought a way to remove values from the realm of criticism. Here he follows the lead of Kierkegaard. Religion and ethical concerns are not subject to philosophical analysis. According to Wittgenstein, one cannot even ask religious or ethical questions. Such answers cannot be put in words, nor can the questions.

But, what about propositions in his writings? Are they nonsensical? Do they make statements about reality? Wittgenstein's response to the propositions made by him are elucidations which cause the reader to recognize that they are nonsensical. By their use the reader is led to climb beyond them. The *Tractatus* should be seen as a ladder to be discarded as soon as it has led one to a correct picture of the world. However, for Wittgenstein, it was the final solution to the problems he considered. Its value consists in showing how little is achieved when these problems are solved. In 1919, Wittgenstein gave up philosophy as well as his inheritance and began teaching children in Upper Austria. Having provided, as he believed, the final solution to the problems of philosophy, he closed the earlier phase of his career as a philosopher. But we shall meet him later with a different proposal.

Next we examine briefly *logical positivism*. By the end of World War I, the Austro-Hungarian empire was destroyed. The only remaining traces of its former greatness were its music, art and learning. It was during this crisis that scientists and philosophers began to hold regular discussions. The group later known as the "Vienna Circle" sought an account of science which included mathematics and sensory experience. Ernest Mach, Moritz Schick, Rudolph Carnap, Kurt Gödel, and Friedrich Waismann were all members of the group.

The thought of the Vienna Circle, called logical positivism, was based upon that of David Hume and Ludwig Wittgenstein. They began by using Hume's empirical criterion of meaning. Hume had insisted that ideas have no meaning if they are not copies of sense impressions. The positivists took this criterion and, using Wittgenstein, modified it somewhat, developing the "verification criterion of meaning."

The positivists asserted that the meaning of a proposition is its method of verification. If one offered the proposition "that cow is brown," one was required to verify it. One could do this by going to the pasture and looking to see if the cow was brown. The proposition meant something about physical cows and the color, brown. The appropriate kind of scientist was then to verify the statement. The philosopher's task was simply to identify whether the proposition was meaningful—that is, whether there was a means by which it could be verified, philosophically.

According to the positivists, two general types of propositions were meaningful: propositions such as "that cow is brown," which could be verified *empirically*, and those such as "all unmarried men are bachelors," which could be verified *logically*. They agreed with Wittgenstein as they looked for names and logical form. They attempted to develop a perfect language that would clearly reflect the world. They also excluded religious and ethical propositions, insisting that propositions about God, being, the good, and so on were meaningless because they were neither logically necessary nor empirically verifiable.

They were influenced by the author of the *Tractatus* in yet another way. The propositions used to describe logical positivism did not meet their own criterion. Their basic assumption, "all meaningful statements must be either empirically verifiable or logically necessary," was itself neither "empirically verifiable" nor "logically necessary." Thus the standard they set up for meaningful propositions was not itself a meaningful proposition. This is, of course, an objective judgment, which did not hinder the adherents to the movement. Its influence continues to be widespread.

Wittgenstein returned to philosophy. He learned much from teaching young students. He discovered, for instance, that the language of children was rich and complex. His students could communicate with each other clearly without knowing anything about the logical form of propositions.

After teaching students, meeting members of the Vienna Circle and informal lecturing at Cambridge, Wittgenstein gained a distaste for formal philosophy. He considered philosophy useless if it did not improve one's thinking about the important questions of everyday life. He ceased to believe in a picture theory of language and began to explore the relationship between language and games. In 1935, he returned to Norway, where he lived in isolation while working on his *Philosophical Investigations*.

The basic thesis of the *Investigations* is that meaningful language occurs in the life of human beings as they do the things that are appropriate. The meaning of a word is no longer dependent upon how it pictures the world. Rather, the meaning of a word is associated with how it is used in the language.

To illustrate his new perspective, Wittgenstein uses the word "game." If we refer to board games, we are aware that they all have something in common. There is a *relationship* between them which makes them all games. These several games have different rules, but there is a relationship between them which justifies the use of language in this case.

Let us now recall an earlier example, "that cow is brown." This proposition must now be analyzed in its *context*. Was the proposition intended to make a scientific observations? Or, was it simply being used to distinguish one cow from another? If it answers the first question, it should employ the language of zoology. It is a part of a language-game associated with scientific observation. If, on the other hand, it answers the second question, the statement is the language-game of farming. In both instances the statement remains *structurally* the same, but a different way of evaluating it is required if it is to have meaning. The statement remains the same, but the meaning is different for the scientist over against the farmer.

Wittgenstein is not seeking a perfect language. The focus is no longer on the logical form of language. It is now directed to the life-situation out of which language arose. All language is suited for the particular needs it serves. Ordinary language is capable of expressing the ideas people wish to convey.

Problems in the use of language arise when propositions are taken out of their particular language-game and applied to a context for which they were not intended. Examples are the use of language to portray "mathematical precision" in history or sociology. Mathematical precision belongs to the language-game of the natural sciences. Liberal arts may be precise, but not in the mathematical sense. Each field has its own language-game. Again, the rules of soccer cannot be judged by the rules of chess, yet both are valid games with proper rules.

Before drawing out the implications of the *Investigations* for ethical and religious knowledge, we need to recall the "picture theory of language" in the *Tractatus*. In the earlier work, Wittgenstein made a distinction between religious and ethical language, on the one hand, and factual language, on the other. Religious and ethical words do not "picture" anything in the world. It is for this reason that they have *no meaning*. They are outside the world of *facts* and therefore outside the world of analysis and critique.

What happens to this distinction in the "game" theory of the *Investigations*? Wittgenstein now allows that such words as *God* and *good* are a meaningful part of language. These words belong to the language-game of religion and ethics. The religious and ethical terms do not need to be *purged* in order to form a more perfect language. Religio-ethical terms are now said to be without meaning if they are taken out of *context*.

It is significant that Wittgenstein held his latter position. It permitted the used of language in speaking meaningfully of religious and ethical questions. His view that the meaning of language is contextual apart from "fixed" understanding is promising for theological reflections. Unfortunately, Wittgenstein ended his life as a confused, depressed and uncertain philosopher, especially in reference to religious and ethical questions. Having rejected his earlier picture theory of language, he was not sure how he could retain the distinction between factual language and religious and ethical language. For whatever reason, he did not publish his *Investigations*.

The principle of verification in analytical philosophy is its most persistent aspect. Because of its strong emphasis upon sense experience, this philosophy has been most successful in the English-speaking world, especially in England and the United States. As we have seen, the outlook can have positive as well as negative results, even for ethical and religious reflection. For instance, its insistence upon the precise use of language, the relation of logic to language and the context of language, among other aspects can be useful.

Concluding Remarks

A discussion of modern trends of philosophical thinking with reference to theological knowledge would be extensive. But the limits of this study indicate the need to bring our present project to an end. We continued our examination of the relation of philosophy to theology begun in the previous chapter. After a brief look at the historical context, we considered the philosophies of process, personalism and language analysis. In each case we took a close look at the life and thought of a seminal thinker. But we also attempted to capture the theory of knowledge, in each instance, for theological reflection.

As I close this volume, I am aware of other equally important persons and movements. For example, recent thought under the caption of "hermeneutics"[11] is valuable for theological discourse. Phenomenology[12] is yet another fruitful area for exploration, and we could go on. But I have completed what I consider an adequate representative study. My purpose has been a modest one, viz., to introduce and demonstrate the profound way in which the development of theology in the Christian West has been undergirded by the encounter with philosophy in every period of history. This theological use of philosophy, in the best manner, continues now and may be expected to be manifest for the foreseeable future.

Notes

I *Introduction*

1. John H. Randall, Jr. and Justus Buchler, *Philosophy: An Introduction* (New York: Barnes & Noble, 1970), pp. 1–10.

2. Diogenes Allen, *Philosophy for Understanding Theology* (Atlanta, GA: John Knox and London: SCM Press 1985), p. iv.

3. George F. Thomas, *Religious Philosophies of the West* (New York: Charles Scribner's Sons, 1965), p. xiv.

4. "Religion" as used here refers to the Christian religion, mainly Protestant and Western. But in a general way it could apply to human religious experience as a whole.

5. Ninian Smart's discussion on "world-views" is global, but see especially his reflections upon "the doctrinal dimensions," in *Worldviews* (New York: Charles Scribner's Sons, 1983), pp. 96–113. Natural scientists resemble philosophy and theology in reference to "worldviews." Observe how shifts in "paradigms" lead to scientific revolutions and new worldviews—e.g. the Copernican Revolution. See Thomas Kuhn, *The Structure of Scientific Revolutions* (Chicago: University Press, 1970), pp. 111–135.

6. See Elton Trueblood, *Philosophy of Religion*, (New York: Harper, 1957), pp. 3–16, who discusses "the necessity of philosophy."

7. *Ibid.*, p. 10.

II *The Early Greek Experience*

1. When I visited Vienna in the summer of 1987, I was preoccupied with the question: why so much genius in one location? The same kind of question arises when one studies carefully the philosophy and culture of ancient Greece. We are here concerned with philosophy and religion—in so far as the two influence each other.

The extensive "note" here on the "Greek experience" is designed to be an invitation to the world of ancient Greece, the context in which the Greek mind developed.

Greeks were concerned about the quality of light. This was true not only during the summer, but during the winter, as well. Bowra writes:

> . . . Even in winter the light is unlike that of any other European country, brighter, cleaner, and stronger . . . The beauty of the Greek landscape depends primarily on light, and this had a powerful influence on the Greek vision of the world (C. M. Bowra, *The Greek Experience*, London: Weidenfeld and Nicolson, 1957, p. 23).

Greek thought is influenced by this light symbolism. Greeks formed a consistent and forthright vocabulary for abstract ideas because their minds, like their eyes, sought naturally what is lucid and well defined. Greek philosophers sought to pin down an idea, define it and make it intelligible.

Plato, for example, in his search for transcendental principles behind the mass of phenomena, tended to see them as individual objects and compared his central principle to the sun which illuminates all things in the visible world, revealing their shapes and colors (cf. *Republic*, vi. 507). The Greeks in their thinking moved from the gifts of the senses to the principles behind them (see Bowra, *op. cit.*, p. 24).

The sea was likewise important to the Greek experience. The mastery of the seas was indispensable for survival. The Greeks were sailors from the dawn of their history. Because they sailed on the seas they were spared a narrow view of life which would have been natural for dwellers in small city-states. For instance, Homer and Aeschylus write about "waterways" or "the laughter of sea-waves." The Aegean was alluring, with its rippling waves and calm. But at times the winds and mounting waves became merciless in their destructive force.

The Greeks learned to live with and reflect upon the unpredictable moods of the sea. The sea provided a lesson on the precariousness of life—as it moved from "a golden calm" to "unforseen disaster." Greek character was shaped by this close encounter with the sea (see *ibid.*, pp. 24–25).

Greek experience provided a basis for unity. Herodotus sums up the characteristics of the Greek experience as a common descent, language, religion and culture. This is a broad conception, which can be illustrated. I close this note with a focus on language.

Greeks had general dialects but one main language. They stressed precise meanings in the use of words. Greek was intended primarily to be spoken. This explains the stress upon clarity in both structure and vocabulary. It was meant to be heard. Therefore, every sentence had to be forceful, carry its full weight of meaning and leave no doubt as to its purpose. The language is flexible— words may assume new duties without losing their freshness and force. Thus Greek is a suitable language for philosophers—it possesses a remarkable capacity for new perspectives and for new persepctives and for speculation (see *ibid.*, pp. 28–29).

2. I am indebted to many sources for the content of this chapter. The reader is directed to these particular passages as resource: Frederick Copleston, *A History of Philosophy* (London: Search Press, 1976), Vol. 1, pp. 1–80; and Frank Thilly, *A History of Philosophy*, Revised by Ledger Wood (New York: Henry Holt and Company, 1952), pp. 7–51.

III *Classical Greek Philosophy*

1. I am indebted to several resources for this chapter. The foremost sources are listed below. Any fallacies in interpretation are mine. Frederick Copleston, *A History of Philosophy*, Vol. I (London: Search Press, 1976), pp. 81–378; T. Z. Lavine, *From Socrates to Sartre* (New York: Bantam Books, 1984), pp. 9–66; Jack B. Rogers and Forest E. Baird, *Introduction to Philosophy: A Case-Study Approach* (San Francisco: Harper and Row 1981), pp. 1–35; Frank Thilly, *A History of Philosophy*, Revised by Ledger Wood (New York: Henry Holt and Company, 1952), pp. 52–119; George F. Thomas, *Religious Philosophies of the West* (New York: Charles Scribner's Sons, 1965), pp. 1–45.

IV *Athens to Alexandria*

1. Stoicism was founded by Zeno, who was born in 336 B.C. at Citium in Cyprus and died in 264 at Athens. His father was a merchant, and Zeno first followed his father's profession. Upon coming to Athens about 315–313, he was influenced by Xenophon, Plato, Socrates and Crates, whom he thought was closest to Socrates. He founded his own philosophic school, which gained its name from the location of his lecturing, the porch (Greek Stoa). This movement was later to have great influence at Rome, where notables like Seneca would be greatly influenced by its insights.

My appreciation of Stoicism and its influence was greatly enhanced by the lectures given by my late mentor, Professor John Baillie of Edinburgh University. Studies in the New Testament as well as Theravada Buddhism and Confucianism indicate a remarkable similarity between these and the ethical insights of Stoicism.

2. Among the Middle Platonists I mention Celsus. Celsus is best known as an opponent of Christianity through Origen's reply to his challenge. Celsus emphasized God's utter transcendence and would not allow that the corporeal is the work of God. To bridge the gulf between God and the world he admitted "demons," angels and heroes. God's providence has the universe as its object and is not, as Christians believe, anthropocentric. See Copleston, *A History of Philosophy*, Vol. I, pp. 455–6.

3. Another comparison is between the sun and the One. Plotinus reflects insights of Plato in *Timaeus* and the *Republic*. It is also instructive to compare this with Christian thinkers who refer to God as "uncreated Light" and creatures as "participated light." Cf. Copleston, *op. cit.*, p. 466.

4. *Ibid.*, pp. 473–5.

5. *Ibid.*, p. 466.

6. For our purpose, the most important follower of Plotinus was Porphyry of Tyre, who joined Plotinus in Rome (A.D. 262). Porphyry made a strong attempt to establish that Plato and Aristotle were in essential agreement. He went beyond Plotinus in his focus upon the practical and religious side of philosophy. Positive religion occupied a crucial part of his interest in philosophy. God, according to Porphyry, is more concerned about deeds than words. Piety is to be expressed through good works. Porphyry is known for his polemics against Christians. He sought to show that Christianity is illogical, ignoble and involved in contradictions. He attacked the Bible and Christian exegesis—he points to the type of insights we now find in higher criticism. The divinity of Christ was a special object of attack, as well as christology in general.

V *What Has Athens to do with Jerusalem?*

1. James Deotis Roberts, *From Puritanism to Platonism in Seventeenth-Century England* (The Hague: Martinus Nighoff, 1968), p. 21.

2. For a discussion of the encounter of Gnostic and New Testament studies, see John Dart, "Fragments from an Earthern Jar: James Robinson and the Nag Hammadi Library," *ChristianCentury*, March 1, 1978, pp. 213–16.

Marcion, whose thought appears radical, was recognized as being within the Gnostic fold. We recall that he rejected Jewish scripture and embraced Paul's epistles and Luke's Gospel as well as other early Christian writings. He even attempted to produce a reconstituted Bible based upon his new understanding. He substituted a gospel of grace for one of law, a saviour for a lawgiver-God. The real issue was that between a creating God and a redeeming God as well as his understanding of salvation in line with the Gnostic view.

3. Among the leaders in this camp were: Justin Martyr (died 166), Irenaeus (born 120), Tertullian (160–240), Cyprian (200–258), Clement of Alexandria (died 216) and Origen (185–254). The movement culminated in the catechetical schools, the first of which was established in Alexandria in 180 by Pantaenus, a former Stoic philosopher.

The purpose of these schools was not only to defend the new religion and demonstrate its reasonableness, but to reduce the teaching to systematic form for the benefit of ministers, who were to instruct non-believers and Jewish converts in the principles of the Christian religion.

Origen was the greatest leader in the Alexandrian school. He worked out a comprehensive theology in which the Neo-Platonic influence was predominant.

I affirm the instructional aspect of this effort by the Apologists, indeed I see this as one important justification for writing this volume. If some persons who need a reasonable interpretation of the Christian faith are convinced of its validity by our discussion, I see this also as an important result, but not as our controlling purpose.

4. We meet in the Apostolic Fathers a type of religion different from Paul's. It resembled Judaism, but was modified by the encounter with Roman law. It was a religion similar to Judaism but more universal. The Epistle of Barnabas, the Didache, and even the Epistle of James, Hebrews and the Apocalypse of John represent this general outlook.

Nomos was central to this stream of Christianity. For instance, in James, faith and works are brought together. These theologians are concerned with divine law as well as human law. The Old Testament is important, as it emphasizes the power of God in his righteousness and justice. This I view as an important dimension of Christian thought. It represents a vital encounter between Christianity and the Greco-Roman ethical tradition.

5. Justin recalls: ". . . I decided to seek out the Platonists, for their fame was great. . . . Each day I advanced and made all possible progress. The perception of immaterial things captivated me exceedingly and the contemplation of ideas gave my mind wings, so that within a short time I supposed that I had become wise and in my stupidity I hoped forthwith to look upon God. For this is the end of Plato's philosophy" (*Dialogue* 2).

6. *Dialogue* 8.
7. *Apology* I. 43.
8. *Apology* I. 46; II. 13.
9. *Against Heresy* IV. 20:5–6.
10. *Against Heresy* IV. 38: 3.
11. Cf. this emphasis upon "deification" in Greek Orthodoxy today.
12. *Against Heresy*, Bk. V.
13. *Against Heresy* V. *Preface*.
14. *Against Heresy* III. 19: 1.
15. *Against Heresy* III. 19: 3.
16. *Against Heresy* IV. 6: 6.

17. *Against Heresy* III. 28: 5.

VI *Augustine and the Primacy of Faith in the Middle Ages*

1. The life of Augustine flows directly into his thought. This is especially true of his theology. In Augustine, theology is autobiography. We will not take up his relation to his mother, his conversion from a life of sensuality, etc. But his doctrines of sin and salvation follow directly from his personal experience of grace, defined as God's undeserved favor. Since Augustine's theology has made an impact on the rest of Christian theology, perhaps more than that of any other single individual, a critical appraisal of his contribution can only come through a thorough understanding of the relation between his life and his thought.

2. *Confessions* III. 4.

3. *Confessions* VII. 9ff.

4. *Confessions* VII. 12, 16.

5. *Confessions* VII. 10, 17.

6. *Confessions* VII. 20.

7. *Confessions* IX. 10.

8. *Confessions* VII. 12.

9. *Prologue* to the Gospel according to John.

10. E. Gilson, *The Christian Philosophy of Augustine* (New York: Random House, 1960), p. 234.

11. *Against the Academics*, Vol. VII, Bk. III, Ch. 11, Sec. 26.

12. *Freedom of the Will*, Bk. II, Ch. 7, 21.

13. Gilson (*loc. cit.*) makes a distinction between the functions of two types of reason in Augustine. He refers to "superior" reason and "inferior" reason. Science is "inferior" reason in this schema, being directed toward the changing world of action.

14. Cf. Copleston, *A History of Philosophy* (London: Burns and Oates, 1956), Vol. II, p. 60.

15. Augustine, *Soliloquies*, I. 12.

16. Gilson, *op. cit.*, pp. 88–92.

17. Augustine, *Sermon* 124.

18. Gilson, *op. cit.*, p. 30.

19. Gilson reminds us that Anselm rather than Augustine is responsible for the formula *credo ut intelligam*. Even so Augustine's mind is behind this assertion. See *Reason and Faith in the Middle Ages* (New York: Scribner's, 1938), p. 24.

VII *The Harmony of Reason and Revelation in the Middle Ages*

1. For Averroes' life and influence, see the following: F. C. Copleston, *A History of Mediaeval Philosophy* (London: Methuen, 1977), pp. 104–24; E. Gilson, *Reason and Revelation in the Middle Ages* (New York: Charles Scribner's, 1938), pp. 37–66. Cf. also Kenneth Cragg, *The House of Islam* (Belmont, CA: Wadsworth, 1975), p. 91.

2. See Copleston, *op. cit.*, pp. 125–149, 181. Cf. Jacob Neusner in *The Way of the Torah* (Belmont, CA: Wadsworth 1988), p. 91. Neusner states that Maimonides was a great Talmudic scholar who was a distinguished physician

and philosopher. According to Neusner, Maimonides brought Neo-Platonic Aristotelian philosophy and biblical revelation together.

   3. *Ibid.*, pp. 176–178.

   4. *Ibid.*, pp. 178–183.

   5. George F. Thomas, *Religious Philosophies of the West* (New York: Charles Scribner's Sons, 1965), pp. 130–131.

   6. E. Gilson, *op. cit.* (n. 1), pp. 80–84. One could continue this discussion almost indefinitely, but this is not desirable. The reader should consult the following sources: Thomas, *op. cit.*, (n. 5), pp. 95–137. This study is very good. A special feature of this discussion is a comparison of Aquinas and Augustine on several important matters. See also Copleston, *loc. cit.* Copleston provides detailed discussion of the use Aquinas made of Aristotle's metaphysics and his doctrine of analogy. This is invaluable (pp. 185–198).

   Our study is limited to representative thinkers. A student of medieval philosophy and theology should spend some time with Duns Scotus and William of Ockham and compare their insights with those of Aquinas. See Julius R. Weinberg, *A Short History of Medieval Philosophy* (Princeton, N.J.: Princeton University Press, 1964).

VIII *Mysticism as Religious Knowledge*

   1. For a look at the basic characteristics of mysticism, see W. T. Stace, *Mysticism and Philosophy* (Philadelphia: J. B. Lippicott, 1960), especially pp. 62, 64. One of the best sources for a comparison of types of mysticism, East and West, is Rudolph Otto, *Mysticism East and West* (New York: Macmillan, 1932), esp. Chap. 4. R. C. Zaehner's *Mysticism Sacred and Profane* (Oxford: Clarendon Press, 1957) is also important.

   2. See M. Hiriyanna, *The Essentials of Indian Philosophy* (London: George Allen and Unwin, 1951), esp. pp. 122–4.

   3. Meister Eckhart, ed. Franz Pfeiffer, trans. C. de Evans (London: J. M. Watkins, 1924–31), *Sermon* I, pp. 4–9.

   4. *Ibid.*, *Sermon* II, pp. 10–12.

   5. See Evelyn Underhill, *Mysticism* (London: Methuen and New York: E. P. Dutton, 1949), ch. 10.

   6. Eckhart, *Sermon* LVI, pp. 23–25, 140, 143. Cf. Tractate XI, p. 366.

   7. Cf. Otto, *Mysticism East and West* (n. 1), pp. 143, 180. See also, Underhill, *op. cit.*, p. 503.

   8. George F. Thomas, *Religious Philosophies of the West* (New York: Charles Scribner's Sons, 1965), p. 157.

IX *Knowledge and Faith in the Modern Period*

   1. It is instructive in the philosophy of science to observe how world-views by scientists, philosophers and theologians converge during the modern period. See Thomas S. Kuhn, *The Structure of Scientific Revolutions* (Chicago: University Press, 2 1970).

   2. See Emile Bréhier, *Contemporary Philosophy* (Chicago: University Press, 1961).

3. John Cottingham, *Descartes* (Oxford: Blackwell, 1986), is one of the best resources on Descartes.

X *Contemporary Religious Thought (I): The Nineteenth Century*

1. Existentialism has many forms. Among existentialists there are perhaps more differences than similarities. However, Kierkegaard, the melancholy Dane, contributed much to giving Existentialism a distinctive character. A host of people, Schelling, Marx, William James, Bergson, Nietzsche, Jacob Böhme and Pascal among them, have contributed to the existentialist theme or mood. Jean-Paul Sartre and Albert Camus gave a brilliant and popular version of this philosophy in their essays, plays and novels. Heidegger and Jaspers gave philosophical expression to it. Existentialism, then, is a mood and mode of thought which may be traced back at least to Socrates, but it has evoked its widest expression in the twentieth century. What these philosophers had in common was a concern about existence, human existence, the conditions and quality of the existing human individual. Christian theologians have naturally been greatly influenced by such an influential movement. Among Protestant theologians, Bultmann, Macquarrie and Tillich are representative. Cf. Samuel Enoch Stumpf, *Socrates to Sartre* (New York: McGraw-Hill, 1966), pp. 453–470.

XI *Contemporary Religious Thought (II): Focus on the Twentieth Century*

1. William James, *Pragmatism* (New York: Longmans Green, 1908), p. 29.
2. Paul Tillich, *Systematic Theology* I (Chicago: University Press, 1951 reissued London: SCM Press 1975), p. 42.
3. See Hugo Meynell, *Freud, Marx and Morals* (Totowa, N.J.: Barnes and Noble, 1981), pp. 107–114. There are other important developments in philosophical thinking during the late nineteenth and throughout the twentieth century which have influenced theology in Europe and America. Phenomenology and hermeneutics are among these. See W. L. Reese, *Dictionary of Philosophy and Religion* (New Jersey: Humanities Press, 1980). "Hermeneutics" is found on page 221 and "phenomenology" on pages 428 and 429. I will mention other trends in due course.
4. George F. Thomas, *Religious Philosophies of the West* (New York: Charles Scribner's Sons, 1965), p. 357.
5. *Ibid.*, p. 365.
6. See Ewert H. Cousins (ed.), *Process Theology* (New York: Newman Press, 1971). Whitehead's doctrine of God is an intellectual challenge. It is a form of dipolar theism which stresses the primordial and consequent natures of God. God is important for the cohesion of his elaborate metaphysical system. See A. N. Whitehead, *Process and Reality: An Essay in Cosmology* (Cambridge: University Press, 1928, and New York: Macmillan, 1929), pp. 519–533.
7. Personalism is relatively recent. Though found in the late nineteenth century, its systematic use belongs to the twentieth century. In France, Charles Renouvier wrote *Le Personnalisme* in 1903; in Germany, William Stern developed critical personalism in *Person und Sache* (1906), and in the U.S., Mary Calkins began to use the term in 1907. Borden Parker Bowne adopted it

in 1908. Bowne considered himself the first thoroughgoing personalist. He left his stamp on the Boston School of personalities.

8. See John Lavely's article in *The Encyclopedia of Philosophy*, ed. Paul Edwards (New York: Free Press, 1967), p. 108.

9. The theologians of personalism (Knudson *et al.*) see Brightman's views on God as in conflict with the best of theological history as well as biblical revelation. They are also aware of evil and suffering, but they have theological responses that Brightman does not have—e.g. the Cross of Christ. Peter Bertocci, Brightman's philosophical successor, is faithful to his mentor on most points.

10. Samuel E. Stumpf provides a good summary of analytic philosophy in his *Socrates to Sartre* (New York: McGraw-Hill Book Co., 1966), pp. 437–452.

11. Richard E. Palmer's *Hermeneutics* (Evanston: Northwestern, 1969) is an invaluable ground-breaking work on the subject of "hermeneutics." He is concerned with the interpretation of texts, i.e. biblical, theological, philosophical and literary texts. Palmer discusses the subject in the American context. He shows how existentialism, phenomenology and literary criticism enrich his understanding. He then takes up theory in Schleiermacher, Dilthey, Heidegger and Gadamer.

12. An excellent introduction to "phenomenology," both as a perspective and as a program of philosophizing, is found in an article by Richard Schmitt. See *The Encyclopedia of Philosophy*, Vol. VI (New York: Macmillan, 1977), pp. 135–151. A bibliography is included.

Select Bibliography

Diogenes Allen, *Philosophy for Understanding Theology*. Atlanta: John Knox, and London: SCM Press, 1985

Karl Barth, *Anselm: Fides Quaereus Intellectum*. London: SCM Press, 1960

Émile Bréhier, *Contemporary Philosophy*. Chicago: University Press, 1961

Edgar S Brightman, *A Philosophy of Religion*. Englewood Cliffs, NJ: Prentice-Hall, 1961

Edwin A. Burtt, *Types of Religious Philosophy*. New York: Harper & Row, 1951

Herbert Butterfield, *The Origins of Modern Science*, New York: Free Press, 1957

Charles E. Butterworth, ed., *Averroes' Middle Commentaries on Aristotle, etc*. Princeton: University Press, 1983

Frederick Copleston, *A History of Philosophy*, Vol. I (Greece and Rome), London: Search Press, 1976

——, Vol. II, London: Burns and Oates, 1956

——, Vol. VIII, Westminster, Md.: Newman, 1966

John Cottington, *Descartes*. Oxford: Blackwell, 1986

Majid Fakhry, *A History of Islamic Philosophy*. New York: Columbia University Press, 1970

Henri Frankfort, *et al.*, *Before Philosophy*. Harmondsworth and Baltimore: Penguin Books, 1964

Étienne Gilson, *History of Christian Philosophy in the Middle Ages*. New York: Random House, 1954

Guttmann, *Philosophies of Judaism*. Chicago: Holt, Rinehart & Winston, 1964

David Hartmann, *Maimonides*. Philadelphia: Jewish Publications Society of America, 1976

Charles Hartshorne and W. L. Reese, *Philosophers Speak of God*. Chicago: University Press, 1965

John Hick, *Philosophy of Religion*. Englewood Cliffs, NJ: Prentice-Hall, 2 1973

——, *Faith and Knowledge*. London: Macmillan, 1974

——, *The Existence of God*. New York: Macmillan, 1964

John A. Hutchison, *Living Options in World Philosophy*. Honolulu: University of Hawaii Press, 1978

Karl Jaspers, *The Great Philosophers*. New York: Harcourt, Brace and World, 1964

Hans Jonas, *The Gnostic Religion*. Boston: Beacon Press, [2]1963

Thomas S. Kuhn, *The Structure of Scientific Revolutions*, Chicago: University Press, [2]1970

T. Z. Lavine, *From Socrates to Sartre*. New York: Bantam Books, 1984

John Mbiti, *African Religions and Philosophies*, Garden City, NJ: Doubleday, 1970

Richard McKeon, ed., *Medieval Philosophers*, 2 vols. New York: Scribner's, 1957–58

Gilbert Murray, *Five Stages of Greek Religion*. Garden City, NJ: Doubleday, 1955

Ian Richard Netton, *Muslim Neoplatonists*. London: George Allen and Unwin, 1982

Richard E. Palmer, *Hermeneutics*. Evanston, IL: Northwestern University Press, 1969

C. H. Perelman, *An Historical Introduction to Philosophical Thinking*, New York: Random House, 1965

Plato, *Theory of Knowledge: Theaetetus and Sophist*. Translator and commentator—E. M. Cornford. Indianapolis: Bobbs-Merrill, 1957

Sarpepalli Radhakrishnan, *History of Philosophy East and West*, 2 vols. London: George Allen & Unwin, 1957

Paul Radin, *Primitve Man as Philosopher*. New York: Dover, 1957

J. H. Randall and Justus Buchler, *Philosophy: An Introduction*. New York: Barnes and Noble, 1971

W. L. Reese, *Dictionary of Philosophy and Religion*. New York: Barnes & Noble, 1981

Jack B. Rogers and Forrest Baird, *Introduction to Philosophy: A Case Study Approach*. San Francisco: Harper & Row, 1981

William I. Rowe and W. J. Wainwright, *Philosophy of Religion: Selected Readings*. New York: Harcourt, Brace, Jovanovich, 1973

Samuel Enoch Stumpf, *Socrates to Sartre*. New York: McGraw Hill, 1966

George F. Thomas, *Religious Philosophies of the West*. (New York: Charles Scribner's Sons, 1965)

David Elton Trueblood, *Philosophy of Religion*. New York: Harper & Brothers, 1957

Julius R. Weinberg, *A Short History of Medieval Philosophy.*
Princeton, N.J.: Princeton University Press, 1964
Alfred North Whitehead, *Process and Reality.* New York: Harper
& Row, 1960